THE ESSENCE OF GOD

Dr. Marie Burkins

Copyright © 2024 by Dr. Marie Burkins

All rights reserved. This book or any portion thereof may not be reproduced or used in any manner whatsoever without the express written permission of the publisher except for the use of brief quotations in a book review.

Printed in the United States of America

First Edition, 2024

PAPERBACK ISBN: 979-8-3302-1692-5
HARDBACK ISBN: 979-8-3302-1694-9
EBOOK ISBN: 979-8-3302-1693-2

Red Pen Edits and Consulting
www.redpeneditsllc.com

DEDICATIONS

I dedicate this book to the countless people God brought into my life, those who have shared so much of Him and His Word with me over the years, which aided in my spiritual growth immensely: to my brothers and sisters in Christ, to my Sunday School and Bible Study teachers, to my Bethesda Theological Seminary professors, and to my pastors.

I dedicate this book to my mother and father, Mr. Willie E. Jackson and Mrs. Cherry A. Jackson, who taught me that I can do anything I put mind to, no matter how big or small the task. They were always my cheerleaders in life.

I dedicate this book to my children, Victoria and William, who I'm so proud to be their parents. They are the apple of my eye.

And last, but certainly not least, I dedicate this book to my husband, Ron. I'm thankful for his endless love and support, and grateful that God allowed us to take this lifelong journey together. "There's a ribbon in the sky for our love".

TABLE OF CONTENTS

Foreword — 1

Introduction — 3

Chapter 1
What Is The Essence Of God? — 5

Chapter 2
God Is Your Kingdom Vision — 9

Chapter 3
God Will Turn Your Trash Into Treasure — 19

Chapter 4
Basking In The Overflow Of God's Graciousness — 29

Chapter 5
God Is The Ground On Which You Stand — 39

Chapter 6
God Is The Fire Burning Inside You — 49

Chapter 7
God Is The Regenerator — 59

Chapter 8
There Is No Failure In God — 69

Chapter 9
    God Is Your Peace   79

Chapter 10
    Redeem The Time With God   89

Chapter 11
    God Is The Key To Your Future   101

Chapter 12
    God Is The House In Which To Abide   113

Chapter 13
    God Is The Declaration Of Truth   123

Chapter 14
    God Really Loves You   133

Chapter 15
    Who Is God To You?   143

Conclusion   153

Resources   163

About The Author   165

FOREWORD

Do you believe in God? Have you ever asked yourself, does God truly exist? I would answer 'yes' to both questions and so would this author, Rev. Dr. Marie Burkins. One more question. Do you want to know about God's character, His essence? Again, if your answer is 'yes', I encourage you to turn the pages of this well written book and find out just who God is, who He is to you and perhaps get to know more about Him.

Just look around to see His amazing creations. This inspiring easy read is packed with demonstrations of His love, His promises, and His nature. Here you will find that God does exist, the essence of who God is and He has the greatest love ever known for mankind.

Through *"The Essence of God"*, Dr. Burkins shines a spiritual light that opens for her readers a pathway leading to God as she explains the attributes of His character and His nature of love as a good Father and compassionate Friend. Dr. Burkins explores throughout these pages God's desire for man to know Him and to share their knowledge of Him with other people.

"The Essence of God" can be used as a tool for anyone who may be the slightest skeptical about God and/or new in their relationship with God. It is also for the seasoned believers

looking for a deeper connection with Him. This author acutely describes the Trinity of God and reveals how salvation is through God's Son, Jesus Christ.

Dr. Burkins is a true friend who has grown in God and in her knowledge of Him. She's a wife and mother of two. She is funny, speaks her mind in love and has an unwavering love for the Lord. She is serious about her walk with Jesus Christ and her work for the Kingdom of God.

Through biblical history and life experiences, Dr. Burkins is a phenomenal teacher who takes her readers down a path making one thirsty for more of God and His unchanging love.

I highly recommend this book, *"The Essence of God"*, and encourage anyone who may be searching for truth or have a desire to grow in their relationship with God. While reading this book, allow your mind and heart to receive its message and experience the true Essence of God.

Tina L. Barnes

Friend and Sister-in-Christ

INTRODUCTION

There are people throughout the world who question the existence of God: Is He real? Who actually knows if there is a God? What evidence can you show me that God exists?

All we have to do is look around at the simple things of life to recognize that God is real and that He exists, even today. Who could produce the sky and the various colors of it? Well, scientists say that it has to do with the number of molecules scattered in the atmosphere, or it has to do with the wavelengths of light in the atmosphere, or it has to do with the distance the sunlight travels to the earth's atmosphere, or it simply has to do with the weather. Regardless of the scientists' answers, the fact is that God exists, and He will cause the sky to be whatever color He deems necessary.

But others who are skeptical about God's existence may ask questions, "How can you believe the Bible?"; "Why do Christians say there is only one way to God?"; "How does one become a Christian?" People everywhere need God. Many are open to considering Him, but they often have questions they want answered before they are willing to accept Christ. As Christians attempt to answer the questions, blending grace with truth, an increasing number of skeptics may give an ear and become seekers or believers.

And yet another group of skeptics may ask, "Why is there evil and suffering?"; "How can Jesus be the only way to God?"; "I could never take the blind leap of faith that believing in Christ requires." God, though sovereign, gave us freedom to follow Him or to disobey Him. This response does not answer all concerns (because He sometimes does intervene to thwart evil) but suggests that the problem of evil is not as great an intellectual obstacle to belief as some imagine. Jesus' plan of rescuing humans (*"by grace ... through faith ... not ... works,"* Ephesians 2:8-9) was distinct from those requiring works, as many other religions do. These two kinds of systems were mutually exclusive. Both could be false or either could be true, but both could not be true. We exercise faith every day. Few of us understand everything about electricity or aerodynamics, but we have evidence of their validity. Whenever we use electric lights or airplanes, we exercise faith—not blind faith, but faith based on evidence. Christians act similarly. The evidence for Jesus is compelling, so one can trust Him on that basis.

This book will recognize the essence of God and will answer some of the questions asked by those who are skeptical of His existence. This book will show that because of God's unchangeable character and attributes, He lovingly intervenes in the lives of so many people because of His constant love for all, which is His overall essence.

CHAPTER 1
WHAT IS THE ESSENCE OF GOD?

The essence of God is the fundamental nature of who He is. His attributes are also identified as His essence. This speaks of His character, His personality. God is in three persons: the Father, the Son and the Holy Spirit. Each has a specific personality and a particular mission. But there is still one God, the Father, the Godhead.

All the characteristics of the divine essence of God are present at all times, but not all are manifest at the same time. Just as while all colors are present in a ray of white light, the individual colors can be seen only under certain conditions of reflection or refraction. Various attributes of God can be seen in certain situations.

For example:

- In salvation, God's love and eternal life are apparent.
- In judgment, His righteousness and justice are manifested.
- In God's faithfulness, His immutability and veracity are shown.

- In God's plan, His omniscience and sovereignty are seen.
- In God's will, sovereignty is paramount.
- In God's revelation, veracity, love, and omniscience are obvious.

Man thinks that God is like him, who is finite, but God is not like man at all. He is infinite, and although the Bible, the Word of God, reveals many of His characteristics and attributes that we can know Him, they cannot be completely communicated to man. His essence can be described to a degree, but they cannot be fully defined. The essence of God is infinite, immeasurable, well beyond man's full comprehension. God is omniscient, whereas man knows only in part. God is omnipresent, whereas man is limited. God is omnipotent, whereas man is weak.

There is no higher knowledge in life than the knowledge of God. It is God's desire that we understand Him and that this understanding give us the courage to conquer, as the heroes of Hebrews 11 conquered, by seeing Him who is unseen (Hebrews 1:27). As we learn to concentrate our thoughts on the essence and the attributes of God rather than on ourselves and our circumstances, we gradually come to realize that we could not possibly ever have a problem that He cannot solve. We begin to understand that we do not always have to know what God is doing. We only have to know that **He** knows what He is doing.

Agape, the love that is part of the essence of God, and as described in 1 John 4:8 and in 1 John 4:16, is nothing like the love that man produces. God's love is part of His eternal Being and thus can never be increased, diminished, or changed. Long before God created anything, love existed among the three Persons of the Trinity (the Father, the Son, and the Holy Spirit). The love that God extends to man is an impersonal love in the sense that it is not based on the goodness or integrity of the person who is the object of love, but on the goodness and integrity of God. God does not love us because of who we are, but because of who He is.

God is Sovereign, as taught in Daniel 4:34–35. God's divine will is above every will. He always has everything under control, and as Creator and King, He is ruler over all His creation.

God is absolute righteousness, perfect goodness. It is impossible for Him to do anything wrong. He is holy and free from sin or wrong. He is guiltless. He is absolutely righteous both in His person (James 17; 1 John 1:5) and in His ways (Romans 3:25–26), and He cannot look upon or have fellowship with that which is anything less than absolute righteousness.

God is absolutely just. It is impossible for Him to do anything unfair. By virtue of His being the Creator, God has the absolute right of authority over His creatures. He has given to man fair and righteous laws which every one of us has broken (Romans 3:23). God's righteousness demands that disobedience against His laws be punished. God's justice fulfilled that demand when God the Son on the cross took the punishment for all men's sin and disobedience. Because of this, God is just (fair and right) to forgive anyone who accepts Christ's provision.

God is immutable, as taught in Hebrews 13:8. He has never changed and will never change. He can neither increase nor decrease. His essence and attributes will always remain the same, no matter what. If we understand this, then we can rest in the fact that no matter how inconsistent or unstable or unreliable we are, God will always be consistent, stable, and reliable.

CHAPTER 2
GOD IS YOUR KINGDOM VISION

*⁸"Now the king of Syria was making war against Israel; and he consulted with his servants, saying, "My camp will be in such and such a place." ⁹ And the man of God sent to the king of Israel, saying, "Beware that you do not pass this place, for the Syrians are coming down there." ¹⁰ Then the king of Israel sent someone to the place of which the man of God had told him. Thus, he warned him, and he was watchful there, not just once or twice. ¹¹ Therefore the heart of the king of Syria was greatly troubled by this thing; and he called his servants and said to them, "Will you not show me which of us is for the king of Israel?" ¹² And one of his servants said, "None, my lord, O king; but Elisha, the prophet who is in Israel, tells the king of Israel the words that you speak in your bedroom." ¹³ So he said, "Go and see where he is, that I may send and get him." And it was told him, saying, "Surely he is in Dothan." ¹⁴ Therefore he sent horses and chariots and a great army there, and they came by night and surrounded the city. ¹⁵ And when the servant of the man of God arose early and went out, there was an army, surrounding the city with horses and chariots. And his servant said to him, "Alas, my master! What shall we do?" ¹⁶ So he answered, "Do not fear, for those who are with us are more than those who are with them." ¹⁷ And Elisha prayed, and said, "L*ORD*,*

I pray, open his eyes that he may see." Then the LORD *opened the eyes of the young man, and he saw. And behold, the mountain was full of horses and chariots of fire all around Elisha."*

2 Kings 6:8-17 (NKJV)

In 2 Kings, chapter 6, there is a story of the King of Aram preparing to go to war with Israel. He would confer with his officers about the plans he'd make, plans to have his army surround a certain city (which was not named), but the plan was to ambush Israel. The King of Aram thought he had the upper hand in this war, until he found out that someone outside of his inner circle heard about all his plans.

Unbeknownst to the king, God had a man in Israel's camp who was in constant communication with Jehovah God. This man's name was Elisha, who was a prophet of the Most High God. The King of Aram's plans were revealed to Elisha by God, and in turn, Elisha would warn the King of Israel. Elisha told the King of Israel not to go anywhere near this certain city because the Arameans were planning an attack, an ambush, against the Israelites. Every time the King of Aram made plans to attack Israel, Israel would find out, through Elisha, and the King of Aram's plans were disrupted. Of course, after so many times of this happening the King of Aram became furious and began to seek out in his camp who was this traitor that was committing high treason.

He was finally convinced that no one in his camp or his inner circle betrayed him. One of his officers told the king that the prophet Elisha was telling the King of Israel their plans, even words the king would speak in the privacy of his own bedroom. You can imagine how extremely angry the King of

Aram was upon hearing this news. So, he ordered his men to go find Elisha, seize him, and bring him back to their camp.

They found Elisha in Dothan. So they went there at night, in secret, got in their places, surrounded the city, and waited for daybreak. When Elisha's servant got up the next morning and stepped outside, he was frightened to see troops, horses, and chariots everywhere! He ran back inside the house to Elisha, frantically told him what he saw, and then asked him "what are we going to do?" Elisha tried to calm down his servant by telling him not to be afraid because "there are more on our side than there are on their side." Then Elisha prayed that God would open the eyes of his servant, to let him see what he couldn't see. And sure enough! God opened the eyes of the servant to see that surrounding Aram's army was another army, filled with horses and chariots of fire. This was the army of the Lord!

When we feel like our backs are against the wall and we feel like we don't know what to do.... when we reach a dead end and figure this is it, I'm stuck, there's no way out.... when we feel like all hope is lost and we just settle for what the world gives us.....this story is proof that God is always working on our behalf!

There are valuable lessons we see in 2 Kings, chapter 6:8-17. First, we have a situation where the enemy, the King of Aram in this case, is trying to destroy the people of God, the Israelites. The Hebrew translation of Aram is Syria, so actually the Arameans are the same people as the Syrians. We read in I Kings 20 where King Ahab of Israel was confronted by King Benhadad of Syria to go to war for all the possessions, including wives and children that King Ahab and Israel had. God made a way for King Ahab and Israel to defeat King Benhadad of Syria.

We also learn about the nation of Aram in 2 Samuel, chapter 8, as having gone against King David and the Israelites, and they were defeated. The lesson to learn here is to be very aware of the fact that as long as you're working for the Lord and you're following His plans, the enemy also has a plan, and that plan is to destroy you. He is not going to give up so easily, just as the King of Aram would not. Although it took him a while to realize that someone was finding out about his plans of attack, he still kept making plans to come after Elisha, until he finally found a way to get to Dothan after Elisha. In the same manner, the enemy, Satan, will not give up trying to destroy the child of God. He is relentless.

But it should also be known that the enemy is a defeated foe, just as he was with King Ahab and with King David, but even more so with the child of God because he walks in the power of God and every weapon that the enemy forms against him shall not prosper--- it will not succeed in its purpose. It must be remembered that the believer does not fight, does not wrestle against flesh and blood but against principalities, against powers and rulers of the darkness of this world. The believer does not fight against spiritual wickedness in high places. Remember that you, as a believer in Jesus Christ, is covered by the blood of Jesus, and that's greater, stronger than any weapon the enemy could ever bring against you!

The second lesson to learn is just as God assigned Elisha to warn the King of Israel about the plans of the enemy (which in this case was the King of Aram), God has His messengers on the lookout for your best interest as His child. When there is danger ahead, God will send a warning that will cause you to avoid any harm. When you just missed being involved in a serious car accident by taking another route to your destination, or when the doctor gives you a bad report on your health, and you're directed to another doctor for a second opinion and that report is more favorable than the first and you're given better treatment by that second doctor; the outcome of these situations do not just happen from good luck, or by your horoscope reading which said, "today is going to be your lucky day!", or "the stars were aligned just right for you", or "you were in the right place at the right time". This is what's called having the favor of God on your life! Psalm 121:5 says that the Lord is our Keeper. He is our covering!

The third lesson to learn is that you have to see what you don't see. When Elisha's servant walked out of the house early the next morning and was stunned to see a large army of men, horses, and chariots surrounding their house and the city in which they lived, he became very fearful, and I would dare say even became like the Apostle Peter, forgetting for a split second where his source of strength and power came from. Like the author Helen Keller, Elisha's servant lost his sight, and he was in the dark, not being able to see the power of God because his focus was fixed elsewhere.

This is one of the easiest ways the enemy can distract the people of God. The believer sometimes tends to focus on what he sees in the natural instead of what he should see in the spirit. In the natural we will see a child getting into so much trouble in school and then conclude that he will amount to nothing in life, end up being a thug, drug dealer, prostitute, in jail, or dead. Instead, we should see in the spirit that the breath of God is in this child and that he is made in the image of God, and because of that he is destined for greatness, that he will become a straight "A" student in school, that he will be surrounded by people who mean him good and not harm, that he will go to college, that he will become a productive citizen in his city, and state, and in this country, and perhaps even the world.

There may be someone who is tied up in so much debt that they don't know how to come from under the big pile of it all. That person's money is looking funny, and his change is strange. The person may lose his job soon, or may have just lost his job with very little or no money coming in. This person may be thinking of taking drastic measures that he knows is wrong, but he can't see any other way out. The caveat is that he must see in the spirit that God's windows of heaven are about to pour out a tremendous blessing with his name on it. He must see in the spirit that God is working things out for his good. He has to see what he doesn't see! He has to use kingdom vision!

And the fourth lesson to learn in 2 Kings, chapter 6:8-17 is that it is so important for the child of God to have a partner who will help him when he becomes weak. Although Elisha's servant was just that, a servant, he partnered with a man who had a strong relationship with the Almighty God. The people of God need to make sure they surround themselves with like-minded people. There are a lot of different kinds of people in this world---very empathetic people who are willing to help at any turn. There are nice people who may treat you to lunch or dinner. There are compassionate people who may give you the shirt off their back. But every empathetic, nice, kind, compassionate person does not have a relationship with God through his Son Jesus Christ. That's who the people of God need to partner with.

When he falls, the man or woman of God need to have someone who will pick him up and restore him back to the Lord God as taught in Galatians 6:1. When he has those times when it feels like all his days are cloudy and dark and no sunshine is in the forecast for him, he need a brother or sister in Christ to encourage him as shown in Psalm 30:5, that "weeping may endure for a night but joy will come in the morning". Although we don't know when morning is coming, we know that it is coming. We just need to hold on and endure to the end of the journey.

We live in a world where the people of God are surrounded by darkness and if we're not focused on the proper sight, it will look like there is no light anywhere to be found. It will look like the enemy has the upper hand in everything and that he wins all the time. But that's a lie! No matter whose name is addressed to 1600 Pennsylvania Ave in Washington, D.C., God is the believer's Provider. Trust Matthew 6:31-32, where Jesus taught "Therefore do not worry, saying, 'What shall we eat?' or 'What shall we drink?' or 'What shall we wear?' For after all these things the Gentiles seek. For your heavenly Father knows that you need all these things."

No matter what laws are passed or not passed, God is the believer's Keeper, as declared in Psalm 121: "I will lift up my eyes to the hills from whence comes my help? My help comes from the LORD, who made heaven and earth. He will not allow your foot to be moved; He who keeps you will not slumber. Behold, He who keeps Israel shall neither slumber nor sleep. The LORD is your keeper; the LORD is your shade at your right hand. The sun shall not strike you by day, nor the moon by night. The LORD shall preserve you from all evil; He shall preserve your soul. The LORD shall preserve your going out and your coming in from this time forth, and even forevermore."

Even when there are wars and rumor of wars, nations revolting against nations, kingdoms against kingdoms, as we see all too well in the news broadcasts today, we choose not to be troubled. Matthew 24:6 encourages us "And you will hear of wars and rumors of wars. See that you are not troubled; for all these things must come to pass, but the end is not yet." Believers in God choose not to be troubled because their eyes are open to see the salvation of the Lord and He is always on their side!

God answered Elisha's prayer and opened the eyes of the servant so he could see what would be revealed only by God alone. The servant was truly able to see that there was much more protection for him and Elisha than there was a plan for their destruction all around them. He was able to see in the spirit the angels of the Lord ready to defend them. He was able to see in the spirit the Lord's horses and chariots, just as the enemy's army had, but God's army consisted of horses and chariots of fire which were symbols of divine power, coming to the defense of those that were surrounded by it, as well as an offense to the enemies who tried to break through it. We must focus on kingdom vision!

Some might think that it was unfortunate that the author Helen Keller had an illness at an early age that took her sight for practically her entire life, and that she had to live in darkness. She had no choice in the matter. But she left behind a beautiful quote: "Keep your face to the sunshine and you cannot see the shadows. It's what the sunflowers do." We, believers in God, need to keep our focus on the SON-SHINE (S-O-N). 2 Corinthians 4:6 states "For it is the God who commanded light to shine out of darkness, who has shone in our hearts to give the light of the knowledge of the glory of God in the face of Jesus Christ." Therefore, let the light of Christ shine in your hearts and stay focused on Him with kingdom vision.

CHAPTER 3

GOD WILL TURN YOUR TRASH INTO TREASURE

"if any man be in Christ he is a new creature; old things have passed away; behold all things have become new."

2 Corinthians 5:17 (NKJV)

Trash day comes in my neighborhood every Thursday. That's also the day that the recycling truck will come. The rule is that residents are not supposed to put the trash and recyclable items in the same container. They're supposed to be separated because there is a distinct difference between the two.

Another term for trash is refuse, which are those items that are no longer wanted or needed, and they are discarded, or rejected. They're thrown out. On the other hand, there are those items that can be recycled, items that were in one shape, one condition, but can be made into something else; items that were used for one purpose but have been made over to serve another purpose.

There are so many people who walk around us, people we don't know and some people we may know, who feel like they are nothing more than trash, refuse, who feel rejected, discarded, no longer wanted. For instance, the person whose spouse left home with no reason and never returned. That person feels discarded.

Or perhaps the child who is ignored by his family, there is no communication, no discipline, no special times together. That child feels rejected and alone.

Or the employee who's been on the job for 30 years or more and one day comes in and is handed a pink slip: "your services are no longer needed". That person is no longer wanted, feels rejected and feels discarded. After all those years with the company, he now feels like trash.

But God is in the recycling business. You've probably heard the saying "one man's trash is another man's treasure". Well, you are a treasure to God. Just as we sometimes see men and women going through trash to find some lost treasure -- perhaps food is the treasure they seek, or money is the treasure they're looking for, or whatever they think is of value to them. God is seeking those who hurt, those who are lonely, those who feel like giving up. Luke 19:10 states "For the Son of Man came to seek and save those who are lost." When we are rejected or dismissed or feel like we are unworthy of someone's company or someone's attention or someone's inner group, we feel lost, confused, and insecure. But every believer need to know that there is HOPE, and in hope we HOLD ON and PRAY EXPECTANTLY. In hope we HOLD ON to His PROMISES which are ETERNAL.

God is going to use these earthen vessels (which are His People), consisting of His special treasure (His Word), to bring about a change in this world. II Corinthians 4:7 declares "But we have this treasure in jars of clay to show that this all-surpassing power is from God and not from us". God is so crazy about us, His children, that He would never treat us like man. He would never discard us, or reject us, or neglect us, or dismiss us. He cares about us so much that He put in this body of clay-dirt a special treasure, which is His Word, which is Jesus Christ, the Word alive. God is so crazy about us that He prepared a place for us well before we were born into his world. He made preparations and plans for us even while we were still in our sins. Romans 8:29 tells us that "He foreknew and predestined us" …. but for what??? "To be conformed to the image of His Son." In scripture, the words "foreknew" and "predestined" go hand in hand, and in the Greek, they mean to "mark out beforehand", or "to appoint beforehand". In other words, God has put a mark on you, knowing that you would come to Him in total belief that He is God, and that Jesus Christ is the Risen Savior.

If God wasn't so crazy about you, He would let you stay in your sinful state and be on your way to Hell. Look at what He did for Jacob. God took a man who was known as a cheater, a deceiver, a conniver, a liar, and changed him into a prince, a fighter, one who prevailed, who became an overcomer by God. Genesis 32:28 speaks "And He said, "Your name shall no longer be called Jacob, but Israel; for you have struggled with God and with men, and have prevailed."

God is so crazy about you that He gave you power to overcome every adversity, every distraction, every trip-up that you got yourself into. He gave you the gift of His Holy Ghost, through His Son Jesus Christ. When you make the wrong decision, or travel down the wrong road, or hang with the wrong crowd and find yourself in serious trouble, God is not like man. He doesn't turn his back on you because you didn't listen to him – NO! He has equipped you with an Advisor to help you in your decision making. God has equipped you with a Protector, who will keep you from spiritual danger. God has equipped you with a Comforter, who will calm all your fears and fill you with hope.

So, God's desire is to recycle His children from something old into something new. His children, having had the veil removed from their faces, are being transformed (being changed) into His image from glory to glory, by the Spirit of the Lord. For instance, take a look at a plain bottle, a plain glass, which has been used and discarded, seemingly good for nothing at all. But an artist doesn't see what it is but he sees what it can become. He sees the potential. He sees the inner beauty that he wants to bring out of it.

So, the artist decides to take that glass and begin a work on it. His aim is to make something beautiful out of what appears to be ugly and even repulsive to some people. There is a very delicate process that the artist will take the glass through but what is interesting about the glass in this process is that it can be made to precision, but it can also be marred, depending on the handling by the artist.

The ugly and repulsive glass must first be pliable, flexible in order for the "newness" to come out of the "oldness". Therefore, the ugly glass must become a molten glass.

The ugly glass will go through very intense heat in a furnace set between 2025 to 2175 degrees Fahrenheit. As it becomes hotter, it becomes flexible for the artist to use, becoming molten glass. A steel tube is used to rotate the molten glass in the furnace to the desired shape. The rotation should be constant, steady, and even. At times the artist will take the glass out of the hot furnace and begin to roll it on a steel table called a marver to get more of the desired shape. Then the molten glass will go back in the furnace for more heat intensity, then it comes out again to be shaped on the marver table. Then there is a time when the artist will blow into the end of the rod, making the heated glass at the other end expand and become like a bubble. This is a continual process until finally, the glass becomes what the artist already saw in his mind. He has recycled an old, discarded glass into a beautiful, one-of-a-kind, useful object. "Old things have passed away; behold all things have become new", 2 Corinthians 5:17.

God is ready to use a very similar process in your life to make you become the beautiful creation He intended you to be. First, he looks at you. He <u>really</u> looks at you, when everyone else has rejected you. When everyone else has discarded you. When everyone else has ignored you. When everyone else has made you feel like trash. He sees the potential and beauty in you. Despite how you may feel: used and abused; broken, busted, and disgusted. He sees far more than anyone else can see, and He wants to display your uniqueness to the world.

Like the glass artist, God will use a once hard product and soften it, so that it will become flexible and submissive in His hands. This will require some intense heat to be turned up in your life, but know that just like the artist, God is constant, steady, and even. "He who is faithful will never leave you nor forsake" (Hebrews 13:5). "He is the same yesterday, today, and forever" (Hebrews 13:8). You may have to go back in the furnace another time, or two, or three, but God is ever-present, right there shaping and molding you into the beautiful creation He designed for His good pleasure.

Subsequently there's the part of the process that comes when you've finally given in to Him, and you're no longer hardened by the cares of this world, you're no longer hardened by anger, jealousy, revenge, selfish ambition. And now that you've become flexible in the Master's hands, He will breathe in you, making Himself come alive in you. You've become the beautiful queen he had in mind from the beginning. You've become the distinguished king he set apart from all others. You can be used for His Glory.

God discards no one, whether society says that Black lives don't matter, whether you've been told that your life means nothing, whether your spouse walked out on you, or whether you feel like giving up and considered taking your own life. God will take the old nature and make you into new creature, but only if you would allow Him to do it. Romans 8:1 teaches us that "there is now no condemnation for those who are in Christ Jesus because the life-giving Spirit of Christ has set you free from sin and death." That means in the Court of Heaven, as a believer in Jesus Christ, you are found innocent right now of whatever accusation that's been placed upon you. Right now, today, you are found not guilty and have no sentence imposed upon you, just as 1 John 3:14 teaches "We have passed from death to life".

Pastor and Evangelist Frederick B. Meyer, who was a friend and contemporary of the famous American Evangelist D. L. Moody, said "it's a terrible thing for a sinner to fall into the hands of his fellow sinners." For example let's briefly look at the woman caught in the act of adultery in the gospel of John 8:1-11 (NKJV):

> *¹But Jesus went to the Mount of Olives. ²Now early in the morning He came again into the temple, and all the people came to Him; and He sat down and taught them. ³Then the scribes and Pharisees brought to Him a woman caught in adultery. And when they had set her in the midst, ⁴they said to Him, "Teacher, this woman was caught in adultery, in the very act. ⁵Now Moses, in the law, commanded us that such should be stoned. But what do You say?" ⁶This they said, testing Him, that they might have something of which to accuse Him. But Jesus stooped down and wrote on the ground with His finger, as though He did not hear. ⁷So when they continued asking Him, He raised Himself up and said to them, "He who is without sin among you, let him throw a stone at her first." ⁸And again He stooped down and wrote on the ground. ⁹Then those who heard it, being convicted by their conscience, went out one by one, beginning with the oldest even to the last. And Jesus was left alone, and the woman standing in the midst. ¹⁰When Jesus had raised Himself up and saw no one but the woman, He said to her, "Woman, where are those accusers*

> *of yours? Has no one condemned you?"* ¹¹ *She said, "No one, Lord." And Jesus said to her, "Neither do I condemn you; go and sin no more."*

We see Jesus doing what He came to earth to do, teach about the kingdom of God. It was the season of the Feast of the Tabernacles, which had just ended, so there was a great amount of people still in Jerusalem. While Jesus is teaching in the church, having everyone's attention, He is suddenly interrupted by a crowd of church leaders bursting into the place. The Bible identifies them as scribes, or teachers of the law, and Pharisees. These were the high-minded preachers of the day, well-educated, well-known men, who were supposed to be full of wisdom and have high moral standards. If anyone had a question about the Law of Moses these were the men to ask. Just imagine someone coming into your church in the middle of a sermon and suddenly interrupting and disrupting the message with matters you have nothing to do with or know anything about. That's what happened in this situation.

These church leaders dragged a woman into the church, and they threw her right in front of Jesus, like a pile of trash, to make sure He saw her, so He would stop what He was doing to pay attention to this situation. The church leaders care nothing about the message that Jesus was giving to the attentive congregants in the church. They aimed to see how Jesus was going to respond to this woman who they felt was no good, was nothing more than trash, and was certainly guilty of a crime that was worth the death sentence. Remember these church leaders are very intelligent in the Law, so they know the Law states that in order to accuse someone of adultery you have to actually see them in the act. They couldn't make the accusation based on seeing them enter a hotel room and then exit the same hotel room. They have to see the couple engaged in the act! These religious men could have tried to help this woman but they didn't want to help her. They wanted to condemn her. They wanted to degrade her. They wanted to destroy her. They wanted to humiliate her because they supposedly had so much respect for the Law of Moses and were more concerned about public morality.

But unlike Jesus they could not give her a new heart and a new life. They could not set her free from wickedness. They could not save her. They could not restore her. Jesus asked the woman where her accusers were after He asked the church leaders to throw the stone of death at her, after having them face their sinful states when asked whoever was free from sin to throw the first stone at her. This caused the church leaders to examine themselves to determine if they were indeed free from any guilt and sin, but everyone left after having been faced with that question, and their conscience got the best of them. Jesus wanted her to catch the realization that everyone was actually gone. Why? Jesus wanted her to know that she was no worse than any of the men who brought her before Him. Jesus wanted the woman to know that although she was caught doing wrong, she didn't have to stay in that wrong. Jesus wanted her to know that there is a valuable treasure within her to be discovered.

Speaking to the disobedient Israelites while they worshipped other gods, Isaiah 64:6 tells them, and these same words apply to us today as well, "All of us have become like one who is unclean, and all our righteous acts are like filthy rags; we all shrivel up like a leaf, and like the wind our sins sweep us away." But PRAISE GOD! He doesn't leave us in that state of uncleanliness, in that state of sinfulness! Yes, God turns trash into treasure, just as 2 Corinthians 5:17 reminds us that "if any man be in Christ (the prerequisite is you have to be in Christ!), he is a new creature; old things have passed away; behold (in other words, watch what Jesus is going to do!), all things have become new."…..so you're free!

Free from condemnation! (To reiterate, Romans 8:1 says "there is now no condemnation for those who are in Christ Jesus").

Free from rejection! (Psalm 94:14 says "For the Lord *will not forsake His people; He will not abandon his heritage"*).

 Free from feeling like trash!

You are now a treasured possession in the sight of God. You must know that coming to God costs you nothing but living for God costs you everything.

But He is in the recycling business, turning trash into treasure, and whom the Son has set free is free indeed!

CHAPTER 4

BASKING IN THE OVERFLOW OF GOD'S GRACIOUSNESS

"And God is able to make all grace abound toward you; that ye always having all sufficiency in all things, may abound to every good work."

2 Corinthians 9:8 (KJV)

There are so many wonderful benefits of being a child of God. We are loved by God more than the greatest man or woman in this world could ever love us. His love is immeasurable and unconditional. God has given us freedom from the heavy load of the law and its condemnation. God has guaranteed His peace within us and all around us, peace that surpasses all understanding. We also have the union of the Holy Spirit within us to lead and guide us each and every day. All of that is just the surface of our relationship with the Father. But who wants to go deeper in their relationship with God? No matter where you are right now, where you come from, you can experience the overflowing of God's graciousness, even today.

As mentioned in the previous chapter, we can look at the life of Mary Magdalene, a woman who was not favored in her community, having a bad reputation among women and men, but Jesus didn't hold that against her. She was a committed follower of Jesus Christ after He rescued her from the hands of her accusers, who wanted to kill her for being caught in the act of adultery. After Jesus was crucified and buried, it was Mary who was the first to discover the Lord's body was not in the tomb where He was laid. After making this discovery, she ran and told Peter and John, who followed her back to the tomb. Once these men saw the evidence that Jesus was not lying there, the scripture says in John 20:8-10 that "they saw and believed, and then went back to their homes". Mary, on the other hand, stayed at the tomb, crying. She was so distraught and wanted answers. She saw two angels in the tomb and asked "where is Jesus' body?" Then she saw another man who she thought was a gardener and asked him also if he knew what happened to Jesus' body. In her moment of grief and despair, she turned, and the one she thought was the gardener was actually the Master Himself, standing before her. In His presence she was able to experience His peace, which calmed all her fears. She was able to experience His love, just by Him calling her name, "Mary".

This is what a personal relationship with Jesus Christ is all about. He will call you by your name, and no doubt that experience changed her life! And from time to time we're given the opportunity to experience the presence of God, especially when we're in a state like Mary, when we are consumed with grief and despair, and we don't understand why certain situations happen to us; when the pressures of this world become too tough to handle and we feel like throwing in the towel and giving up; when we feel like walking out on a marriage, or walking off a job, or running away from home; when we feel like we're unloved and unwanted, and look for a way out, even if it means popping a bunch of pills that will dumb you down, or drinking so much alcohol that you don't know which way is up. God will make His presence known just at the right time, just when we need Him the most.

All that is well and good, but what if there is more to just being in His presence for that short period of time. What if we're able to dwell in His presence , to be enveloped in Him, to really rejoice in Him? That's what it means to bask in Him, so much so that we become consumed by Him, where there is an overflow, a spilling over, a running-over of Him in you, and it is noticeable to everyone.

If you truly have a relationship with Jesus Christ, you already have a flow of His anointing, and you're being set apart for his service. You already have a flow of His grace, of His favor. But do you want the minimal flow? You know, just enough to get by, just enough to say, "I'm saved". Or do you want more of Him, an overflow of Jesus, an overabundance of Jesus in your life? So much so that you will follow the scripture in John 14:12, where Jesus said that "you will do greater works than Me because I will go to the Father", or like Elisha told Elijah in 2 Kings 2:9 "I want a double portion of your spirit (or power)", or like James 4:6 says that "God gives more (or greater) grace"?

God is extraordinary. He has no boundaries, and He is looking for his sons and daughters to be extraordinary and do extraordinary things. And in order to do so you have to seek an overflow from Him, pursue more of Him in you.

Let's consider the Shunamite woman found in the Word of God in 2 Kings 4:8-38. Here is a woman who was wealthy, living with her husband, in a town called Shunam. The prophet Elisha would travel through this town from time to time, and the woman would invite him to her house for dinner. After some time she and her husband decided to build a room specifically for Elisha so that when he came through town he would be able to stay in their house. They furnished the room with a bed, a table, a chair, and a lamp. All the comforts of home. The woman was very kind and very generous to Elisha and his servant, knowing that Elisha was a true man of God. Elisha wanted to show his appreciation by giving her something. So he told her how much he and his servant appreciated her kindness and hospitality, and asked her if there was anything he could do for her, anything she may want, even perhaps put in a good word of her to the king, but her response was "no". She wasn't looking for anything in return. What was in her heart manifested in her actions. She had kindness in heart. She had love in her heart. She had humility in heart. These are qualities we don't typically see from a wealthy person. But because of the way she treated the anointed man of God, God was going to reward her. And he did it in a way that she never imagined.

During those days, the status of a woman was low on the totem pole of society. There were very few women mentioned in the Bible who actually had money and wealth. For her to be called a wealthy woman was probably due to her husband's work. So although they had everything money could buy, there was still one thing she didn't have and this thing was very important to a woman in that society, and that was that she didn't have a child. Like Hannah and Sarah, she was barren. But unlike these women, we don't see in the Word of God that she prayed for a child. But that's ok because God knows the heart of all of His children.

Perhaps there are some desires that you've kept to yourself. Not only have you not mentioned them to anyone, you've not even prayed about them to God. You can rest assured that God knows your heart, and if you really love Him, and treat people the way they should be treated, and be obedient to Him, God will reward you openly.

So, in spite of her telling Elisha that she didn't want anything from him, he told her anyway that in a year she would be holding a son in her arms. Note that Elisha didn't say she would be holding a child. He was very specific to the sex and said she'd be holding a son. This is very significant because in those times, it was important for a woman to have a male child, to be an heir to the father's inheritance, and so of course, this woman was elated. And because this woman displayed the fruit of the Spirit, as outlined in Galatians 5 (love, joy, peace, patience, kindness, goodness, faithfulness, gentleness, and self-control), demonstrating the character of God, she received an overflow of God's kindness, blessings, and graciousness. The scripture said that her husband was an old man, so she was probably an old woman too, past childbearing age. But God can make what seems to be impossible possible! There is an overflow of God's blessings when you display His character as the Shunammite woman did.

Scripture in 2 Corinthians 9:8 states "And God is able to make all grace overflow to you so that because you have enough of everything in every way at all times, you will overflow in every good work". There is a seed that God has planted in you. That seed is His Word. He is expecting you to take care of it, to cultivate it, nurture it, so that it will grow, it will multiply, and He will bring increase. And as He brings the increase, you will grow in righteousness. And as you grow in righteousness, you will be able to share God's generosity. Again, you will grow in righteousness and generosity, two of the many undeniable qualities of Jesus Christ that every child of God should grow and mature in, to strive to possess.

Let's consider the life of another woman found in Luke 7:37 who is referred to as a sinner. Before coming to the Pharisee's house, she was already familiar with Jesus, having been delivered from seven demons. And her appreciation towards Him never wavered, even when she was an unwelcomed guest at the Pharisee's house. The Pharisee didn't want her there, thinking to himself that Jesus surely couldn't be a prophet nor was he sent from God if he wanted to associate with this sinful woman. Jesus knew the heart of this man and He dealt with him, but the overflow of Jesus' love and compassion towards this woman was so tremendous that it caused her to weep, bow down, and wipe His feet with her hair, and kiss His feet, while anointing His feet with expensive perfume.

Have you ever felt the love and compassion and grace and mercy of God so greatly in your life that all you could do is cry? Perhaps while driving down the road and thinking about the love of God, or washing dishes and cleaning the house, or working in your yard, and you see the beauty of

God's creation all around you, and you begin to think about what God has done for you and how He has brought you through this, that, and the other thing? Then you begin to weep. That's the overflow of God's graciousness!

Jesus said in John 15:7 "if you abide in me and my word abide in you…." That's dwelling or basking in the love of God.

Apostle Paul said in I Corinthians 3:7 that "neither he who plants is anything, nor he who waters, but God who gives the increase". God doesn't want you to stay at the minimal but to increase in everything He has for you - to overflow in God's graciousness!

John 10:10 lets us know that "the thief does not come except to steal, and to kill, and to destroy." Jesus said "I have come that they may have life and that they may have it more abundantly". God doesn't want you to live a mediocre life but He is ready to bring an overflow, an overabundance of life to you.

But being obedient is the key. Then you will receive the reward. Just as Malachi 3:10 says to "bring all the tithes into the storehouse, that there may be food in my house, and try me now in this, says the Lord of hosts, if I will not open for you the windows of heaven and pour out for you such blessing that there will not be room enough to receive". Readers of the Word of God tend to take the last portion of the scripture and run with it. Don't skip over the first part of scripture! Be obedient to the entire scripture of God's Word and watch how He will bring increase in your life. He even invites you to try Him, to test Him at his Word, and see if He's for real or not.

David was a man after God's own heart and he learned of the overflowing graciousness of God as he wrote Psalm 23, declaring that the Lord will make his cup to run over. Run over with what? God will make David's cup, David's vessel, David's life to overflow with His provision, with His safety, with His care, with His personal relationship, with His goodness, with His mercy. But for how long? All the days of David's life!

King Hezekiah learned of the overflow of God's graciousness when he was healed from his illness and God blessed him with 15 more years of life, after Isaiah pronounced death upon him at the age of 39 years old.

Even in the Old Testament, in Deuteronomy 1:8-11, on God's behalf, Moses told the Israelites that God had given them the land and they only needed to go and possess it. This is the land that God swore to Abraham, Isaac, and Jacob, the land that was flowing with milk and honey. Moses went on to tell them that God brought the increase of these people. God multiplied the people. Even when they were enslaved in Egypt God brought increase, and now their population is innumerable, just like the stars in the sky. Hebrews 11:6 clearly states that "you must believe that God is and that He is a rewarder of those who diligently seek him."

2 Corinthians 3:4-6 (Amplified Version) teaches us: "Such is the confidence and steadfast reliance and absolute trust that we have through Christ toward God. Not that we are sufficiently qualified in ourselves to claim anything as coming from us, but our sufficiency and qualifications come from God. He has qualified us [making us sufficient] as ministers of

a new covenant [of salvation through Christ], not of the letter [of a written code] but of the Spirit; for the letter [of the Law] kills [by revealing sin and demanding obedience], but the Spirit gives life." Whatever overflow of God's graciousness that comes into your life is not of your own doing. It is God who does the work in you and through you, according to His perfect will, and you are not to take credit for any of it. Your sufficiency, your qualification, your abilities, all come from God.

You are a part of the Abrahamic covenant if you believe that God is who He says He is, and if you believe Jesus Christ is the Son of God. Being a part of the Abrahamic covenant gives you access to all the promises of God. So, just as there was an overflow in the lives of the children of Israel, in their population, in their possession of the land that God prepared for them, you have access to the same promises of overflowing blessings today. Overflowing increase in your household. Overflowing increase on your job. Overflowing increase in your finances. Overflowing increase in your ministry. Overflowing with good health. Overflowing with beautiful family relationships. Overflowing of God's graciousness.

No matter what comes your way, just know that you are a phenomenal Queen and you are a phenomenal King. You are a royal priesthood. You are a chosen generation. You are a holy nation. You are a peculiar people, especially appointed, hand-crafted, and molded by God. You have been called out of the darkness into His marvelous light. Never let the negativity tell you any different. There's nothing that will be able to tear you down. There's nothing that can stop you from succeeding, because you bask in the overflow of God's graciousness.

CHAPTER 5

GOD IS THE GROUND ON WHICH YOU STAND

> [13]*"But we are bound to give thanks to God always for you, brethren beloved by the Lord, because God from the beginning chose you for salvation through sanctification by the Spirit and belief in the truth,* [14]*to which He called you by our gospel, for the obtaining of the glory of our Lord Jesus Christ.* [15]*Therefore, brethren, stand fast and hold the traditions which you were taught, whether by word or our epistle."*
>
> *2 Thessalonians 2:13-15 (NKJV)*

Until the unfortunate and tragic death in 2012 of Trayvon Martin of Florida, I never heard the term "STAND YOUR GROUND". It was during this event that I learned that if you fear that your life is in imminent danger, you can use deadly force as a means of self-defense. In using the law, STAND YOUR GROUND, an individual can avoid prosecution if the courts believe the individual legitimately applied it in self-defense, even if it means taking the life of the assumed perpetrator. In the African American society, the death of Trayvon Martin took us to a place where we haven't been in a long while. The life of Black men, as well as Black women, is taken for reasons that don't make sense at all. Taken because one individual deems another human being's life unworthy to breathe the same air or walk the same streets. A life where people in power can make decisions about certain groups of people they feel they can control in any way that suits their fancy. However, the same terminology Satan use to bring destruction and despair in families, the same terminology the children of Satan use to manipulate the minds of individuals they deem unnecessary to be alive, or they deem unfit to live in a better country or to have a better job, the same terminology can be used for the kingdom of God, and that is to <u>STAND YOUR GROUND</u>!

  This is a country supposedly founded on Christian values, but where is the evidence of that? Where are those values when we have people in legislative positions who are not for all the people, although they've been elected by the people? Washington, D.C. is gearing up for the next presidential election in 2024 and the line of people throwing their hats in the ring is steadily getting longer. And we have to be careful of those who want the Christian vote. Jesus said in Matthew 7:15 that we should "beware of the false prophets, who come to you in sheep clothing but inward are ravenous wolves." Jesus knew there would be people going about who would endeavor to spread the gospel, claiming to be a Christian who love Jesus, but they ultimately have ulterior motives. This is the biblical equivalent of "fake news". Paul admonished, or reprimanded, the Galatian church in Galatians 1:6, saying to them "I am astonished how quickly you are deserting the one who called you by the grace of Christ and are turning to a different gospel." The church needs to be careful and stand your ground!

Paul is teaching the believers in Thessalonica in 2 Thessalonians 2:13 that they are morally obligated to always give thanks to God because He chose them and they accepted His call to salvation, through repentance, faith, and obedience, through the renovation of the heart and mind, and to believe in His truth. They were to hold tightly to these truths and their beliefs.

Even today, as Christians, we are called to stand firm on what we've been taught in the Word of God. There are groups today claiming to be Christians, followers of Jesus Christ, when in actuality they are merely cults, having nothing to do with Christian values at all. Paul taught his son in the ministry Timothy in 2 Timothy 4:3 that "the time will come when men will not tolerate sound doctrine, but with itching ears they will gather around themselves teachers to suit their own desires" (Berean Standard Bible). Another translation says "they will gather around them a great number of teachers to say what their itching ears want to hear" (NIV). Some people don't want the truth. Those who preach a false doctrine understand this and understand that there is an audience for "Christianity-lite". You know, like the juice Minute Maid Lite, or the lemonade mix Crystal Lite. The point is that they are not authentic. They're watered down from the original version. They lack substance. The church must STAND YOUR GROUND!

Be aware that there are false prophets who teach watered down, fake versions of the Holy Scriptures that suit what their audiences want to hear. They remove the parts of scriptures that aren't convenient to one's lifestyle. They promote a different lifestyle than the one taught by Christ. And if you're not careful you will be easily deceived. That's why you have to stay on guard at all times. You must scrutinize what you hear and what you read against the true authority, which is the Word of God as found in the Holy Scriptures.

Well, you may ask: "how is it possible to stand your ground when so much confusion, disruption, disappointments, hurt is breaking loose in so many families, on people's jobs, and even in some churches?" The answer can be found in Ephesians 6:10-17:

> *"10 Finally, my brethren, be strong in the Lord and in the power of His might. 11 Put on the whole armor of God, that you may be able to stand against the wiles of the devil. 12 For we do not wrestle against flesh and blood, but against principalities, against powers, against the rulers of the darkness of this age, against spiritual hosts of wickedness in the heavenly places. 13 Therefore take up the whole armor of God, that you may be able to withstand in the evil day, and having done all, to stand. 14 Stand therefore, having girded your waist with truth, having put on the breastplate of righteousness, 15 and having shod your feet with the preparation of the gospel of peace; 16 above all, taking the shield of faith with which you will be able to quench all the fiery darts of the wicked one. 17 And take the helmet of salvation, and the sword of the Spirit, which is the word of God;"*

You have been given the proper equipment to stand fast, to stand firm, and to stand your ground when the enemy and his crew come to destroy you. You have the upper hand because you have all you need to destroy him. It's not about the bullets, or knives, or cannons, or even your fists. It's all about the Word of God, the Sword of the Spirit, which is a fire extinguisher, extinguishing every piece of fire Satan and his crew throws at you! Yes, stand your ground! Face the devil!

Have you ever noticed that there is not a piece of armor mentioned in verses 10-17 which covers your back? That's because you're not supposed to run away. God's got your back! The latter part of Ephesians 6:18 tells us to stay alert with all perseverance. James makes it very clear to us, in chapter 4:7, that we are to submit ourselves unto God, resist the devil, and he will flee.

It needs to be understood that in order for you to stand your ground you first must have a solid foundation on which to stand. So, the next question is what foundation are you standing on? In Matthew 7:24-27 Jesus gives an illustration of two types of foundation a person can build a house on: a foundation that is as solid as a rock, so that when the torrential rains fall and beat so hard against the house; when the high winds blow so hard it feels like the house is going to collapse; when the rough and tough times of life come hitting you hard and you feel like hiding your face in the sand; when you have so many sleepless nights and you just can't catch a break. If your foundation is sure, and is built on the Solid Rock which is Jesus, then you can stand your ground successfully. The scripture says that person is WISE.

But if you've chosen to be foolish, as the scripture says, and build your house on sand, then you will have the opposite results. When the torrential rains fall and beat so hard against the house; when the high winds blow so hard it feels like the house is going to collapse; when the rough and tough times of life come hitting you hard and you feel like hiding your face in the sand; when you have so many sleepless nights and you just can't catch a break. If your house is built on a foundation that is on sand, then your house will fall and be completely destroyed, and you will go out of your mind!

You must understand that the house that is being built is you. You determine the foundation on which you stand. You determine what to do with the many violent, torrential temptations Satan bring your way. When the flood waters come, when the fire gets hot, you determine the choice of whether you will stand or whether you will fall. We have a promise from God in Isaiah 43:2 (NKJV) that says "when you pass through the waters I will be with you; and through the rivers, they shall not overflow you. When you walk through the fire, you shall not be burned, nor shall the flame scorch you." The Good News Translation says it this way: "when you pass through deep waters, I will be with you; your troubles will not overwhelm you. When you pass through fire, you will not be burned; the hard trials that come will not hurt you." If you, the house, is built on a solid foundation, God's got you!

Galatians 5:1 from the Contemporary English Version reads "Christ has set us free for freedom. Therefore, stand firm and don't submit to the bondage of slavery again." Don't allow the cares of this world that which you were pulled from, the pit you dwelt in, don't let those things put you back into slavery, under the subjection of Satan. You will fall, but you get back up again. Proverbs 24:16 tells us that "a righteous man (or woman) will fall seven times and get back up. But when the wicked fall, they are brought down by calamity." You may have slipped and fallen back into a drug habit or in a drunken state....GET UP AND STAND YOUR GROUND. God will raise you with His righteous right hand!

In spite of what Doubting Thomas or Sour Sally have to say, that your faith is not strong enough because you fell, or you may have been stricken with a disease or illness where you have to go through some radical medical treatments, or the illness may have the doctors puzzled and they say they don't have a cure, don't look at the situation as a death sentence but as an assignment from heaven, where you will have to be like some to win souls for the Kingdom, as Paul wrote in I Corinthians 9:22 NIV: "To the weak I became weak, to win the weak. I have become all things to all people so that by all possible means I might save some." Stand your ground. You know what God has put in your spirit. You are free to be used by the Master, so go forth in His power and in His might.

Consider Job's wife. Because of all he went through, losing all his wealth and all his 10 children, as well as becoming terribly ill, she told him to curse God and die. She didn't understand the plan of God in Job's life, and initially Job didn't get it either but he ultimately came to that conclusion when he declared "though He slay me yet will I trust Him." At some point Job must have realized that this was an assignment for him to go through for God to be glorified. So, stand your ground. Everyone is not going to understand your walk and your God-given purpose.

There is a reward from heaven for standing firm for the Kingdom of God. Ephesians 4:8 states that "Whereforth he saith, when he ascended up on high, he led captivity captive, and gave gifts to men." In this scripture Paul was referring to the ancient custom of conquerors, where the conquering King would lead his enemy captive, bound in chains, marching them before the people in celebration of his victory. The victorious king would bring home the spoils of the defeated kingdom and as the people lined the streets in celebration of the king's return in victory, he would throw gifts of the spoils to the people. Colossians 2:15 tells us that "having spoiled principalities and powers, he made a shew of them openly, triumphing over them in it."

What does this mean for us today? Because of the death and resurrection of Jesus Christ, and because he has triumphed over all His enemies, which is Satan, sin, and death, and because He has ascended high, led captivity captive and gave gifts to men, we can stand our ground and celebrate the fact that He has made us victorious and triumphant in all things. HALLELUJAH!

George Zimmerman killed Trayvon Martin because he believed his life was in danger. He felt threatened by this young man because he couldn't see his face. It's reported that George Zimmerman and Trayvon Martin wrestled on the ground before the child was killed. That is George Zimmerman's defense in standing his ground. The people of God have the same defense. Stand your ground against your enemy, which is Satan. Your life is in danger because Satan is out to steal from you, kill you, and destroy you. If you have a true sincere relationship with Jesus Christ, Satan is threatened by you because he knows he will be destroyed by God himself. You won't have to wrestle with the enemy because you have the Sword of the Spirit which is the Word of God, and that's the best weapon you could ever use to destroy the works of the enemy. Sometimes it's hard to see Satan and his tactics clearly but stand your ground, put on the full armor of God daily, as taught in Ephesians 6:13. Be diligent in prayer, fellowshipping with the saints of God, study His Word. That way you won't be caught off guard when Satan comes to attack.

The eyes of the Lord are roaming the earth seeking the lost who want to be found, seeking the lame who want to be healed, seeking the bound who want to be delivered, seeking those who want restoration. Be encouraged that you can have it. Just stand your ground. As long as you stand your ground God will uphold you with His righteous right hand. Don't compromise your integrity by going along just to get along. Don't cheat people. Paul commands in Romans 13:8 "Pay your debts as they come due. However, one debt you can never finish paying is the debt of love that you owe each other. The one who loves another person has fulfilled Moses' Teachings." (God's Word Translation)

Don't give up, don't give in to the attractions of this world, and don't give in to the trickeries of the enemy. You stand on the solid ground which is Jesus, all other ground is sinking sand. "Your hope is built on nothing less than Jesus' love and righteousness. You dare not trust even the sweetest frame but wholly lean on Jesus' name. Even when darkness veils His lovely face, you still rest on His unchanging grace. Even in every high and stormy gale, your anchor holds within the veil. And when He shall come with trumpet sound, oh may you then in Him be found dressed in His righteousness alone, faultless before the throne." Why? Because "on Christ the solid rock we stand and all other ground is sinking sand!"

CHAPTER 6

GOD IS THE FIRE BURNING INSIDE YOU

⁷"O Lord, You induced me, and I was persuaded; You are stronger than I, and have prevailed. I am in derision daily; everyone mocks me. ⁸For when I spoke, I cried out; I shouted, "Violence and plunder!" Because the word of the Lord was made to me a reproach and a derision daily. ⁹Then I said, "I will not make mention of Him, nor speak anymore in His name." But His word was in my heart like a burning fire shut up in my bones; I was weary of holding it back, and I could not."

Jeremiah 20:7-9 (NKJV)

There was a popular commercial on TV back in the 1970s and 1980s that had the catch phrase, "when EF Hutton talks people listen". EF Hutton was a well-respected stock brokerage firm that had a great reputation for managing mutual funds and other financial investments. The commercial usually centered around a conversation between two people in a room full of other people. The two people are talking about advice from their stockbrokers, when one person would ask the other, "who is your broker?", and the other person would answer "EF Hutton and he said….", and before this person could complete his sentence, everyone else in the room stops what they're doing and draws closer to the conversation to hear just what EF Hutton would have to say.

Jeremiah was not into the stock markets, but he was someone who had a lot of speaking engagements and he tried to give people good advice from God. The problem is that people didn't treat Jeremiah like they would EF Hutton. People wouldn't stop in their tracks and listen to Jeremiah. They would <u>hear</u> him, but they wouldn't <u>listen</u> to him.

Jeremiah was the last prophet of God to the nation of Judah, the southern kingdom of Israel, and he fervently preached to them to repent and turn away from their idolatry. He went through severe challenges and difficulties in his ministry: God instructed him not to marry and have children and his friends turned their backs on him. So, he was terribly lonely since he had no comfort or companionship from anyone. He was beaten and thrown into prison, then put into an empty cistern that had no water in it, but it had a thick layer of mud at the bottom of it that Jeremiah sank into – all of this from being bold enough to say what the Lord told him to the tell the people of Judah, which was to save them from utter destruction.

The nation of Israel, just like many nations today, had stopped putting God first and had replaced Him with false gods. Like them in that manner, today we put our careers before God; we put our children before God; we put our material possessions before God; we put our money spending before God; we put all our fleshly desires before God. Just like the nation of Israel, we'd rather look to our false gods for comfort, satisfaction, joy, peace, forgetting that everything we have comes by the grace of God, everything we have comes by the compassion of God, everything we have comes by the mercy of God.

God had delivered His people from bondage in Egypt, had performed miracles before them, and had even parted the waters of the Red Sea for them. In spite of all these displays of God's power, they returned to the false practices they had learned in Egypt, including turning their allegiance to the Queen of Heaven, a Mesopotamian goddess of love and fertility. So, God finally turned them over to their idolatry, telling them in Jeremiah 44:25, "Go ahead and carry out your promises and vows to her".

Jeremiah was given the task of delivering an unpopular, convicting message to Judah, one that caused him great mental anguish, as well as making him despised in the eyes of his own people. In 1 Corinthians 1:18, God says that His truth sounds like "foolishness" to those who are lost, but to believers it is the very words of life. God also said in 2 Timothy 4:3-4 that the time will come when people will not tolerate the truth.

The people of Judah in Jeremiah's day did not want to hear what he had to say, and his constant warning of judgment annoyed them. And this is so true of the world today. Believers have a responsibility to follow God's instructions of warning the lost and dying world of impending judgment. Even though most are not listening, believers must still persevere in proclaiming truth in order to rescue some from the terrible judgment that will inevitably come.

But in his anguish, Jeremiah got to the point where he said in essence, "Enough is enough. I'm not going through this persecution from my own people anymore. I'm tired of being hurt and full of pain. I try to help these people and they turn and laugh at me, make jokes about me. I have no family or friends I can talk to or vent to. I have no one who can truly understand and relate to what I'm going through. What's the point? No one is listening and no one cares. God, I'm done!"

When you feel discouraged in ministry and you feel like giving up and want to turn your backs on your God-given calling, when you want to throw in the towel and tell God "Thanks but no thanks", you must remember the same words of encouragement that God gave to Jeremiah in chapter 1:17-19 (NLT): "Get up and get dressed. Go out and tell them whatever I tell you to say. Do not be afraid of them or I will make you look foolish in front of them. For see, today I have made you immune to their attacks. You are strong like a fortified city that cannot be captured, like an iron pillar or a bronze wall. None of the kings, officials, priests, or people of Judah will be able to stand against you. They will try, but they will fail. For I am with you, and I will take care of you. I, the Lord, have spoken."

Jeremiah had a brief moment of despondency, giving way to the feelings of his flesh. And that's what we do. You know that old saying: "if you can't stand the heat, get out the kitchen!" or "I'm coming apart at the seams!" But these feelings last only for a moment, just as with Jeremiah. This was not his entire life's character. Jeremiah realized that as much as he wanted to renounce the calling on his life, he more-so had to proclaim the Word of God because he was on fire! In essence, in verse 9 of chapter 20, He said that he couldn't contain the urgency that he felt. He couldn't keep his mouth shut because the power of the Word was so strong in his inner being that he felt like he was going to explode. He had to release it from himself. He had to get it out!

There are other witnesses in the Bible who were on fire as well and they couldn't keep quiet. We see the Apostles Peter and John who went before the religious council of priests and Sadducees. These church folks wanted Peter and John to stop proclaiming the good news of Jesus Christ. What really got these disciples in trouble was that they also preached about the resurrection of Jesus Christ which the Sadducees didn't believe in. But many people who heard the good news believed and were saved anyway, about 5,000 people, not including women and children. Peter and John were asked to leave town and no longer spread this propaganda and they replied to the council in Acts 4:19-20: "Do you think God wants us to obey you rather than him? We cannot stop talking about the wonderful things we have seen and heard." They couldn't keep the Word to themselves because they were compelled to preach wherever they went!

Another person who was on fire for the Lord was Apostle Paul in I Corinthians 9:16: "For though I preach the gospel, I have nothing to glory of: for necessity is laid on me; yes, woe is to me, if I preach not the gospel!" Paul had a calling on his life directly from Jesus Christ, and he knew that there was a power within him that overwhelmingly compelled him to preach the gospel. Even if he wanted not to do it, he couldn't because of the urgency he felt to do the work of the Lord.

Paul said in Romans 1:14-15, "I am under obligation both to Greeks and to barbarians, both to the wise and to the foolish. So, I am eager to preach the gospel to you also who are in Rome." He was ready, being on fire, to preach the saving grace of Jesus Christ to everyone, rich or poor; intelligent or ignorant. The fire inside of him wouldn't let him do otherwise.

We see the woman at the well was on fire and she didn't use the water bucket she had to douse out the fire either! What began as a simple conversation with a man she felt shouldn't be talking to her in the first place, His words turned into an internal volcanic eruption within her, and she couldn't be still. She had to run and tell everyone what just happened to her. And although people had preconceived ideas and made conclusions of her personality, preconceived ideas of the type of woman she was, preconceived ideas of what she may have been doing in her personal life, they couldn't deny the fact there was something different about her. An important note to remember from this incident: don't ever dismiss the messenger of God. The person you think is not worthy of your time is the very person God will use to set you free from any bondage you may be in.

The last witness of being on fire for the Lord was the leper in Mark 1:40-45. This man came to Jesus with a horrendous, incurable skin disease that made him an outcast. The signs of leprosy are as follows and are most likely what this man experienced: it begins as small red dots on the skin. Before too long the spots get bigger and start to turn white, with a shiny or scaly appearance. The spots soon spread over the body and hair begins to fall out, first from the head, then even from the eyebrows. As things get worse, fingernails and toenails become loose; they start to rot and eventually fall off. Then the joints of the fingers and toes begin to rot and fall off, piece by piece. Gums begin to shrink, and they can't hold the teeth anymore, so each tooth is lost. Leprosy keeps eating away at the face until the nose, the palate, and even the eyes rot, and the leper wastes away until he or she dies.

This disease was so horrific that according to the Jewish law this man was not allowed in the temple nor was he allowed to be with his family, or any part of the working or social society. He actually had to live outside of the city with other diseased, rejected people like him. He was completely excommunicated from all familiarity. But although he was excommunicated from everyone, he knew about Jesus, and he had the confidence that He had the power to heal and completely cleanse him from this disease. By the time this man comes to Jesus he is in the latter stages of the leprosy disease, for this story is also told in Luke's gospel, chapter 5:12, which states "the man was full of leprosy." This man's whole body and life was rotting away. He hadn't had the care, compassion, nor touch of another human being in such a long time. But when Jesus touched him, that all changed! When Jesus spoke to him with compassion, He was instantly transformed! When Jesus healed his body from this horrible skin disease, that altered this man's life! When Jesus restored this man's dignity, Jesus was the man!

And Jesus was glad to do this. However, Jesus also honored and respected the Jewish law, which said that when a person is healed from an infirmity he must first go to the priest, who would examine him, conduct a ceremony, and then pronounce him clean, and then he was able to go back to his family and live back in society with others. But because this man appreciated the major impact Jesus made on his life, he had to be disobedient to Jesus' command. He couldn't go to the priest, at least not right away. This man was on fire! He couldn't keep to himself what the Lord had done for Him. The sudden healing! The sudden deliverance! The mercy shown towards him! Instead of running to the priest, he went running all over town, showing everyone the new person he had become! Mark 1:45 (American KJV) said "he went out and began to publish it much, and to blaze abroad the matter." If he were here today, he would write at least a two-page article in the State Newspaper, in the New York Times, in the Washington Post, in The Chicago Times, as well as pull all the fire alarms in all the office buildings he could get to, to get everyone's attention to hear about the man who changed his life forever!!

So now the question becomes: Are you on fire? Do you feel compelled to share the gospel of Jesus Christ? Do you feel fire in your innermost being so strongly that you have to shout to the world the saving power of Jesus Christ?

Have you ever been in a place in your mind, or even said in words, where you said you weren't going to do this or that for the Kingdom, knowing without a doubt that you heard the instructions from God? But then God put such an urgency in you that you had to release it? You had a burning desire to move, to speak?

Just like EF Hutton need good, active investment brokers, God need investment brokers or agents too for His Kingdom. God need men and women who will invest their time, talents, and energy in spreading the Gospel of Jesus Christ, people who have a burning heart's desire to advise people on how to get to know Jesus. You don't need to worry about the people's reactions. In John 6:44 Jesus said, "No one can come to me unless the Father who sent Me draws them." That is to say that God draws with his Word and the Holy Ghost. Man's duty is to hear and learn, to receive the grace offered, and consent to the promise.

Don't be discouraged like Jeremiah was, when people ridicule you or ignore you. In the words of my former pastor, Rev. Bobby L. Smith, you'd have the "can't help its". If you're fulfilling the calling on your life, if you're doing the work you know God has called you to do, in spite of crazy looks from people wondering why you do what you do, in spite of jokes being made about you, calling you the oddball, you have the "can't help its". You can't help but to work for the Lord because of the burning fire inside you that won't let you rest. You have the "can't help its" to go wherever God leads you to preach to a dying world, even if you're the first and only preacher in your family. You have the "can't help its" to weep over lost souls, like Jeremiah did, knowing what their end will be. You have the "can't help its" when you know God has called you to go to out and minister to the homeless, even if you go by yourself. You have the "can't help its" when you know God has called you to minister in the foreign missions field, even when your family tells you that you shouldn't go anywhere overseas, as unsettling as the world is right now. You have the "can't help its" because of that burning fire inside you that will not let you rest. You've got to move... you've got to speak...you've got to sing....You've got to shout

HALLELUJAH! PRAISE THE LORD, recognizing how good God has been to you, recognizing how God's mercy and grace has kept you throughout all your years, throughout the good, the bad, and the ugly!

So, there is an urgency, to "be steadfast, unmovable, always abounding in the work of the Lord, and know that your labor will not be in vain". Everyone has a choice, whether to hear and heed, or turn a deaf ear. It's not your job to make people make up their minds. It's your job to fan the flame within you, and for that flame to begin a fire, and that fire burns so much inside your bones that you will have no other choice but to move, to speak, to proclaim the blessings of the Lord. That burning fire within you will cause you no other choice but to cry loud and spare not, as said in Isaiah 58:1. That burning fire will cause you to follow Isaiah's instructions in chapter 40:9: "You who bring good news to Zion, go up on a high mountain. You who bring good news to Jerusalem, lift up your voice with a shout, lift it up, do not be afraid. Say to the towns of Judah, "Here is your God!" Jesus said in John 12:32 "If I be lifted up from the earth, I will draw all men unto me". Be on fire for the Lord! Just open your mouth and see the Word work in mighty ways!

CHAPTER 7
GOD IS THE REGENERATOR

¹ In the seventh month, on the twenty-first of the month, the word of the Lord came by Haggai the prophet, saying: ² "Speak now to Zerubbabel the son of Shealtiel, governor of Judah, and to Joshua the son of Jehozadak, the high priest, and to the remnant of the people, saying: ³ 'Who is left among you who saw this temple in its former glory? And how do you see it now? In comparison with it, is this not in your eyes as nothing? ⁴ Yet now be strong, Zerubbabel,' says the Lord; 'and be strong, Joshua, son of Jehozadak, the high priest; and be strong, all you people of the land,' says the Lord, 'and work; for I am with you,' says the Lord of hosts. ⁵ 'According to the word that I covenanted with you when you came out of Egypt, so My Spirit remains among you; do not fear!' ⁶ "For thus says the Lord of hosts: 'Once more (it is a little while) I will shake heaven and earth, the sea and dry land; ⁷ and I will shake all nations, and they shall come to the Desire of All Nations, and I will fill this temple with glory,' says the Lord of hosts. ⁸ 'The silver is Mine, and the gold is Mine,' says the Lord of hosts. ⁹ 'The glory of this latter temple shall be greater than the former,' says the Lord of hosts. 'And in this place I will give peace,' says the Lord of hosts."

Haggai 2:1-9 (NKJV)

There is an online article in the Huffington Post by a contributing writer named Justine Brooks Froelker, where she writes: "*Stop starting over; begin again.* At the heart of it, these words are the true spirit and essence of ever upward." She goes on to say that "Every time we start over, we also attempt to erase our past or erase us or at least parts of us." She says "I know many of us are struggling to forgive ourselves of our past mistakes or struggles or regrets. Or we wish we had done something differently in the past. But when we look to erase these parts of our story or completely start over, we don't honor who we are today."

At some point in our lives we've all done something or even said something that we've regretted and wanted to completely erase it like it never even happened. But think about it. That situation or those words eventually brought you to a better place. You learned not to make the same mistakes. You learned to watch more carefully the words that come out of your mouth. In the end it was all good because it made you a better you.

In the very short Old Testament book of Haggai (it only has two chapters) we meet a prophet of God. He has been given the assignment to speak to the governor of Judah, Zerubbabel, as well as to the high priest Joshua. The Israelites, who had just returned to Jerusalem from their 70-year captivity in Babylon, was to begin work on rebuilding the temple in Jerusalem that had been destroyed by the Babylonian armies. Upon their return to Jerusalem they began their work, and they finished laying the foundation of the temple. They were so happy with this accomplishment because the elders remembered the former temple that King Solomon constructed, in all its beauty and splendor. They rejoiced and rejoiced with their shouting and weeping altogether, so much so that it was heard in far off distances.

But they stopped there. For 10 years they did no more work on the rebuilding project. Haggai told the people that God was looking for them to complete their work. They made excuses because they were initially afraid. Their neighbors tried to deter their work, acting like they wanted to help with the project when in fact they wanted to keep an eye on the Israelites to make sure they wouldn't become strong. But Zerubbabel saw right through them and told them that they were not a part of this assignment. It was only for them, the Israelites, to finish.

Then the enemies tried to bribe some of the Israelites to go against the plans of rebuilding. However, that plan didn't succeed. The people of God must know that the enemy is always around making plans to abort the purpose of God for His people. The job of the people of God is to stay alert and to keep in mind 1 Peter 5:8 where we are warned to "be sober, be vigilant; because our adversary the devil walks about like a roaring lion, seeking whom he may devour."

But still no work was being done to rebuild the temple. The Israelites became sidetracked in their own personal priorities. They took more interest in building and beautifying their own homes, planting their own gardens, wearing their fine clothing, having plenty of their own food, all the while forgetting about their purpose.

You see, the temple of Jerusalem was an extremely important part of the Israelite culture. This was the place that represented the presence of God. It was their focal point in their relationship with God. But they allowed outside influences (fear of their enemies) and inside influences (self-indulgences) to interrupt their purpose and their assignment.

God told them thru the prophet Haggai that all they do, all they try to accomplish on their own, will be a waste because they are neglecting Him. While they are living high on the hog and got their bling-bling in the house and cars and clothes and refrigerators full, they will never really be satisfied. They will make plenty of money but will have holes in their pockets. They won't be able to keep money and won't understand why or where it's going.

In essence God said in chapter 1, verses 9-10, that everything they gain He will take away because they neglected His house and left it in ruins. They forgot who protected them and kept them even while they were in captivity. They forgot about the one who gave them favor in the sight of King Cyrus of Persia to release them from captivity to go home to Jerusalem. They forgot about God! The people of God need to make sure they put their priorities in the proper order. Let's not get so caught up with keeping up with the Jones' and forget about keeping up with the things of God!

When we read the stories about the Israelites, we think they're so bad and so awful to have disobeyed God in such a terrible way. But how different are we than them? How often do we put more emphasis on making sure we have the right house, on the right side of town, in just the right subdivision, on just the right street? How many of us make sure we have the right name brand clothes, and forget about the one who made provisions for us to live the luxurious life? We forget about the one who made provisions for us to have income to make the purchases to live the glamorous life. Are you putting more emphasis on all of what you're getting instead of putting emphasis on the One who got you?

How many of us get so caught up in our feelings when we're hurt? Someone said a mean word to us in church. Or we said a mean word to someone in church. Or someone caught you doing something that would be considered ungodly to the family of God. Now your name has become the subject of this week's gossip page in the church news gazette.

Don't let these distractions, brought to you by the enemy, deter you from your God given assignment and purpose. The job of the enemy is to shift your focus away from God. Don't get in a position like the Israelites, where you've accumulated so much and have gotten caught up in the affairs of the world, just to have it blown away because you neglected your Source of all things. The enemy came to them in different ways to stop their work project but their leader, Governor Zerubbabel, had the mind of God when he told them "No, it's a project only for the people of God." How many of you really have the mind of Christ, strong enough to tell Satan to move out of your way when you know you're working in God's plans? Or do you give in to the persuasive sweet talk when Satan comes your way? Don't forget, he deceived Eve in the Garden of Eden with his sweet talk and flowery words, ultimately causing Eve and Adam's relationship with God to drastically change.

Remember 1 Peter 5:8 warns us to "be sober, be vigilant; because your adversary the devil, as a roaring lion, walks about, seeking whom he may devour." You've always got to be on your toes, never knowing when the enemy will come, or in what way.

In Haggai 1:11 the Word says that "God called a drought". That sounds pretty bad, doesn't it? That God would call a drought to threaten the livelihood of His people! To have a drought come to the land was very detrimental to the livelihood of the Israelites. They could grow no crops, and their animals would suffer and possibly die of starvation. To have God cause your livelihood to suffer doesn't sound like a loving God, does it? But just like our parents disciplined us to get us back in line with what is right, God's purpose is the same and sometimes it takes extreme measures to get our attention, and to get us back in line with His will and His purpose for us. But bless the Lord that He still loves us and is faithful towards us in spite of how we treat Him! He gives us an opportunity to <u>begin again</u>!

When Gov. Zerubbabel, the high priest Joshua, and all the people heard the message of God, Haggai 1:12 states that they obeyed the Word, and they worshipped the Lord with true sincerity and seriousness. These people made a choice. They could have stayed where they were and tried to keep moving on up on their own like the Jefferson's or they could have heeded to the Word, which is what they did. And what was God's response? In verse 13 He encouraged them: "I am with you." In chapter 2, verse 4, He said it again in case they didn't catch it the first time: "I am with you." He told them to "be strong, be courageous, I've got you! Just do the work. Fulfill your assignment. I'll take care of everything else." Because you will find that when you begin again, you'll see that this time will turn out much better than the last time.

That's what God said in verse 9, that the latter building will be greater than the former. When we are born into this world, we're given a house that is in a world of sin, which makes us sin bearers, based on the decisions made by our fore-parents, Adam and Eve. That's what Psalm 51:5 teaches us, that "we were born a sinner, even from the moment our mother conceived us." But we can begin again by getting a new house, one that is only received by being born again. And although we are still <u>IN</u> a world of sin, we are no longer <u>OF</u> this world of sin. Our residence is not made with hands but is eternal. According to 2 Corinthians 5:17 we've begun again, from sinners (the old building) to saints (the new building). God shows Himself to be The Regenerator.

The Word also said in Haggai 2:9 that "peace will be in the new place." With Jesus Christ we have that peace in our new building. Isaiah 9:6-7 the Word states that "His name will be called Wonderful, Counselor, Mighty God, Everlasting Father, Prince of Peace. Of the increase of His government and peace there will be no end." God shows Himself to be The Regenerator.

When we begin again, we have a new building, the temple of the Holy Ghost. When we begin again, we have peace that surpasses all understanding. When we begin again, we have God's security and protection. When we begin again, we have all the provisions of God. God shows Himself to be The Regenerator.

Ezekiel 36:24-28 states "For I will take you from among the nations, gather you out of all countries, and bring you into your own land. Then I will sprinkle clean water on you, and you shall be clean; I will cleanse you from all your filthiness and from all your idols. I will give you a new heart and put a new spirit within you; I will take the heart of stone out of your flesh and give you a heart of flesh. I will put My Spirit within you and cause you to walk in My statutes, and you will keep My judgments and do them. Then you shall dwell in the land that I gave to your fathers; you shall be My people, and I will be your God." It is God's will that you partake of all the benefits of beginning again. God shows Himself to be The Regenerator.

Don't stay in disobedience. Turn around and begin again. Don't think that your situation is so bad that you can't begin again because God is waiting and ready just for you with open arms to receive you. Don't let past mistakes keep you from missing out on the love of God. Don't let negative, critical words deter you from moving up and onward in your calling.

He's asking you to do what He told the Israelites to do - work. And he will do the rest. Work out your salvation with fear and trembling. Work while it is day, for night is coming when no man can work. In all the work you're given, do your best as if you are working for the Lord not an earthly master. When the Israelites began again, and were obedient and worshipped God, that's when their whole world changed. Increase came. Protection from their enemies was given. Prosperity in their land abound.

Learn from your past mistakes and failures. That's a part of what brought you to this place. Don't erase them. That's your history. Just don't stay there. Reach for the future. Do the work, as said in Philippians 3:14 to "press toward the goal for the prize of the upward call of God in Christ Jesus." When you press you are pursuing, you're aggressively chasing something. In this case you want to aggressively pursue, chase the prize which is Heaven as your eternal home.

Don't get stuck in a rut. You don't need to wait for a clean slate. God is in the business of making all things new. His healing brings restoration beyond understanding, no matter where you come from or what you've done. You can begin again. He is The Regenerator. God speaks in Isaiah 43:18-19, in the Voice Translation: "Don't revel only in the past or spend all your time recounting the victories of days gone by. Watch closely-- I am preparing something new; it's happening now, even as I speak, and you're about to see it. I am preparing a way through the desert; waters will flow where there had been none." God is calling you to let go of the "former things" in your life so you can cling to your new identity in Christ.

Lamentations 3:22-24 declares "Because of the Lord's great love, we are not consumed, for His compassions never fail. They are new every morning; great is Your faithfulness. I say to myself, "The Lord is my portion; therefore, I will wait for him." Though we may face difficult times, God renews His grace in every situation we face. You can begin again! The word of the Lord lets us know that every moment brings a fresh start, a new beginning in God through Jesus Christ. God has made and is making all things new, and this includes you.

You don't have to start over. That gives the idea that you would go back to the starting point again and again to get it right. It's like you're at the starting point of a race. You leave your starting block too soon, before the starting gun is shot, so you have to go back to the starting block and start all over. You go back to start over again and in your anxiousness and excitement, you start too soon again so you have to go back and start all over again. You keep making the same mistake and you're told to go back again and again to start over until you get it right. So eventually you don't get anywhere because you're concentrating on starting over to get that thing right!

You don't have to start over with a new strategy. You don't have to rethink on how you can do it better. You don't have to think twice or three times over on how to move in a different direction. Just be diligent in your pursuit to begin with Christ Jesus, right where you are! Revelations 22:17 encourages us to "Come. And let him that heareth say, Come. And let him that is athirst come. And whosoever will, let him take the water of life freely." God has shown Himself to be The Regenerator.

CHAPTER 8
THERE IS NO FAILURE IN GOD

[14] "And when He came to the disciples, He saw a great multitude around them, and scribes disputing with them. [15] Immediately, when they saw Him, all the people were greatly amazed, and running to Him, greeted Him. [16] And He asked the scribes, "What are you discussing with them?" [17] Then one of the crowd answered and said, "Teacher, I brought You my son, who has a mute spirit. [18] And wherever it seizes him, it throws him down; he foams at the mouth, gnashes his teeth, and becomes rigid. So, I spoke to Your disciples, that they should cast it out, but they could not." [19] He answered him and said, "O faithless generation, how long shall I be with you? How long shall I bear with you? Bring him to Me." [20] Then they brought him to Him. And when he saw Him, immediately the spirit convulsed him, and he fell on the ground and wallowed, foaming at the mouth. [21] So He asked his father, "How long has this been happening to him?" And he said, "From childhood. [22] And often he has thrown him both into the fire and into the water to destroy him. But if You can do anything, have compassion on us and help us." [23] Jesus said to him, "If you can believe, all things are possible to him who believes." [24] Immediately the father of the child cried out and said with tears, "Lord, I believe; help my unbelief!" [25] When Jesus saw that the people came

running together, He rebuked the unclean spirit, saying to it, "Deaf and dumb spirit, I command you, come out of him and enter him no more!" [26] Then the spirit cried out, convulsed him greatly, and came out of him. And he became as one dead, so that many said, "He is dead." [27] But Jesus took him by the hand and lifted him up, and he arose."

Mark 9:14-27 (NKJV)

Have you ever been stuck in a situation where you couldn't see any way out? Where it seemed like every possible answer seemed to make matters worse? We tend to focus on what we can't see happening, and eventually hopelessness takes over. When our current circumstances look bleak, it's easy to forget God's past promises.

I was having a discussion with a friend who felt hopeless about his life and was to the point where he wanted God to take his life from here just to be relieved from his suffering. He lived high on the hog at one point in his life, making big money. But things changed, circumstances occurred that caused a major shift in his life and all the good times became bad, and the bad times lasted for many years. Now although he says he believes in God, he feels that God is not listening to him nor cares about his situation, and he prefers to just throw in the towel and give up on life. Despite your circumstances, no matter how rough it is, no matter how ugly and dirty things may be, know that there is no failure in God!

The scripture reference in Mark is about a father who is desperate to save his son's life. He went to people who he believed could help him, Jesus' disciples, God-fearing men who had been with the most influential man around. A man who had gone about healing the lame and sick, restoring sight to the blind, and performed so many wonderful miracles. Surely, the father thought, since these men ate, drank, slept, travelled with Jesus, at least one of them could help his son in the same way Jesus helped so many others. Here is a father who may have gone to many physicians before, trying to get the help his son needed. Here is a devoted father who couldn't stand to see his son tortured and tormented by an evil spirit. And also notice that he included himself in the tortured experience, as he asked Jesus "to have compassion <u>on us</u> and to <u>help us</u>". This father was terribly grieved along with his son throughout this awful ordeal. At this point in the scripture, he may have felt there was no hope left in this situation. He may have felt like throwing in the towel and just let his son die. At least he would be out of his misery. But he wanted to try one more thing. From all the things that he heard Jesus had done for others, he may have gotten the idea that by going to Jesus there will be no failure in his circumstances. And just as he had hoped, Jesus did not fail him. Even when it looked like that evil spirit had won, and it looked like the count was out, and the boy looked like he wasn't going to get up, because everyone said he was dead, Jesus fixed the fight, revived the boy, and he lived!

Psalm 20:7 reads: "Some trust in chariots and some in horses, but we trust in the name of the LORD our God." You must understand that seeing isn't believing when it comes to the Lord, just as 2 Corinthians 5:7 instructs us to "walk by faith and not by sight". It may seem easier to trust in tangible things around you, but God's love, grace, and mercy are the only things that are truly trustworthy.

Let me give you another example of some people who learned that there is no failure in God. There are two widowed women mentioned in the Old Testament scriptures, Ruth and Naomi. Ruth is the daughter-in-law, and Naomi is the mother-in-law. Ruth was married to one of Naomi's sons. Both women lost their husbands in a relatively close span of time. In those days a woman's worth was based on her husband's worth and when he died, she was basically left vulnerable, weak, and helpless. So, Naomi and Ruth faced a life of despair. But God fixed that situation in such a way that Ruth left her godless family and her familiarity in Moab and moved to Bethlehem with her mother-in-law Naomi, which was her hometown. God fixed their situation where Ruth would eventually meet a good Godly man named Boaz, and together they would have a son named Obed, who would have a son named Jessie, who would have a son named David, who would ultimately become king of Israel, and from which our Savior Jesus Christ was born. Ruth and Naomi ended up with riches well beyond their wildest dreams. So in spite of Ruth and Naomi feeling sorrowful about having lost their loving husbands, and in addition to that Naomi lost her two sons, in spite of them feeling empty and in despair, God turned their circumstances around to show that in Him there is still no failure!

We're taught in Joshua 1:9 to "be strong and courageous. Do not be frightened, and do not be dismayed, for the LORD your God is with you wherever you go." The Good News we learn from this verse, and even in Ruth and Naomi's situation, that with God on our side, we have nothing to truly fear.

One more example of someone who learned that there is no failure in God is found in the book of Judges, chapter 6. This is where we meet a man named Gideon who is hiding in caves from the Midianites, a nation of people that God brought against the Israelites because of their disobedience towards God in practicing idolatry. The Midianites were a cruel bunch of people. Whenever they would see the Israelites plant their crops, these people would come and attack the Israelites, taking all their food, sheep, oxen, donkeys, leaving them with absolutely nothing at all. The Israelites were left to starve to death. So, they cried out to the Lord and in His compassion and mercy, He heard them and answered. God sent an angel to Gideon, who was threshing wheat in a hidden place away from the sight of the Midianites. The angel of the Lord called him a "mighty man of valor", which he certainly didn't see himself as being, and gave him the assignment to overtake the Midianites and all the other raiders who had been oppressing the people of God for many years. After seeking confirmation from God that this is truly his assignment, Gideon was ready to move. However, there was a problem with the number of men he planned to bring to this war. Gideon called 32,000 men from four tribes to join his army, but God cut that number down to 300. He wanted Israel to know that when victory came, it would be by the hand of God and no one or nothing else. Ultimately, God fixed the situation where Gideon and his army did not have to fight the Midianites and their alliances after all. When Gideon and his army blew their ram's horns for battle and broke their clay jars at the edge of the Midianite's camp, God caused panic and confusion among the Midianites and their alliances, to the point where they fought against each other with own their swords, in the end killing each other. And for those who were not killed, they fled to the mountains where they were later captured and killed.

What is amazing about this story is that Gideon probably thought he'd have to do a lot of planning to defeat the Midianites. He probably mapped out a great strategy in his mind of what he was going to do and where he was going to place his men for the battle. But in the end he didn't have to do anything at all. He didn't even have to draw a sword! All he did was stand and watch! That's what verse 21 of chapter 7 reads from the New Living Translation Bible, that "each man stood at his position around the camp and watched as all the Midianites rushed around in panic, shouting as they ran".

Here again we see that there is no failure in God! Just as the Word of the Lord was spoken to Governor Zerubbabel as Judah was coming out of Babylon, preparing to rebuild the temple in Jerusalem, we must remember that our triumphs are "not by might, nor by power, but by My Spirit, saith the Lord of hosts." God said in Psalm 90:2 that "before the mountains were born, before you gave birth to the earth and the world, you were God. You are God, from everlasting to everlasting."

The saints of God need to remember that the same power that raised Jesus from the dead is the same power that lives in you today, according to Romans 8:11, where the Word says, "But if the Spirit of Him who raised Jesus from the dead dwells in you, He who raised Christ from the dead will also give life to your mortal bodies through His Spirit who dwells in you." Therefore, the same power that raised Jesus from the dead, that same resurrection power can bring new life to your marriage, can bring new life to your family, can bring new life to your finances. That same resurrection power that raised Jesus from the dead can heal your body from high blood pressure, can heal your body from diabetes, can heal your body from cancer, and can heal your body from any other disease the doctor wants to speak over you. That same resurrection power can bring new life to your walk with Christ, new life to your calling, new life to your ministry, new life to your anointing.

This same principle applies not only to our seasoned saints but also to our youth and young adults as well. The same resurrection power that raised Jesus from the dead is the same power that will help our youth and young people do well in school, whether they are in a virtual classroom or in person at school. If they truly study with intensity, the Holy Spirit will bring total recall to their memory bank and once pen is put to paper, they will ace that test, or that project. That same resurrection power will help our youth and young people find good friends, who will add to their life, not bring damage or destruction to their life. That same resurrection power will help them find the mate they may be looking for, at the appropriate time. Even in that, there is no failure in God!

Yes, life gets hard sometimes, and we try our best to make it easier, but even with our best efforts we still fail. We think of every plan known to man to ease the pain, to bring our plans to fruition, but we eventually fall short. Why? Because we don't always seek God's directions. Proverbs 14:12 lets us know that before every person lies a road that seems to be right, but at the end of that road is destruction and death.

You were created in the image of God. Therefore, you are of God and your agenda should be of God, and once you are God-centered, no weapon fashioned against you, or words spoken against you, or any schemes that are planned to come against you, none of them will work. Know in your spirit that He is a Way Maker. He is a Miracle Worker. He is a Promise Keeper. He shines as a Bright Light even in the midst of darkness. From the rising of the sun until the going down of the same, God is from everlasting to everlasting. He does not change and there is no failure in Him!

Referring back to Mark 9, verse 23, Jesus has basically given all of us the key to unlock these feelings of hopelessness, despair, fear and weakness, when He said to the boy's father that "if you believe then all things are possible." The point is that for you to really know that there is no failure in God you must first believe, and as Hebrews 11:6 teaches us, that you "must believe that He is God, and that he is a Rewarder of them that diligently seek Him." Nothing is too hard for God. In spite of Ruth's upbringing in Moab, a place where idolatry is practiced and there is no reverence for the true living God, and because of Naomi's influence, she eventually believed. In spite of Gideon's fear of the Midianites and how he had to hide in caves from them, knowing they could utterly take him and his people out, he eventually believed. And in spite of this father seeing his son's life being tormented and tortured day after day after day, he eventually believed.

The Word of God declares in Hebrews 13:8 that "God is the same yesterday and today and forever". Besides that, He said in Malachi 3:6, "I am the Lord, I change not". Furthermore, James 1:17 declares that "every good gift and every perfect gift is from above, and comes down from the Father of lights, with whom is no variableness, neither shadow of turning". Add to that 2 Samuel 7:28 where we read "Sovereign Lord, you are God! Your covenant is trustworthy, and you have promised these good things to your servant." God's Word has stood the test of time. It is uncompromising and unadulterated. It is pure, flawless, enduring, eternal, and true. It can be your shield and source of everything you need.

My friend ultimately did not end his life, nor did he walk away from God. Like some of us, he had a moment of despair, believing that his situation was going to be permanent, that nothing was going to change. Perhaps like the desperate father of the suffering son, my friend thought that his unfortunate circumstances were his lot in life. But then he discovered that his trials and his difficulties were a test of his faith. He learned that he had to be patient and to allow patience to have her good work. He learned that his circumstances were meant to cause him to grow and mature in the Lord and be complete in Christ. In the end, he had a Job-like experience. God restored what he lost: he regained his income, even more than what he originally had. He gained a renewed confidence in God; his faith in God was increased; his maturity in Christ was greater. He learned that after all was said and done, there is no failure in God.

There is no failure in God because we serve a resurrected Savior. There is no failure in God because we believe He causes us to triumph in all things. There is no failure in God because we are confident that the good work that He began in us will be carried on to completion until the day of Christ Jesus. There is no failure in God because He wants to do something new in you. He will make a pathway through the wilderness and will create rivers in dry wastelands. There is no failure in God because we believe in the blessed hope that there will come, someday, a new heaven and a new earth, and that the kingdom of God will reign and triumph. There is no failure in God because we believe our hope is not in our own abilities, nor in our goodness, nor in our physical strength. We believe that "our hope is built on nothing less than Jesus' blood and His righteousness. We dare not trust the sweetest frame but only lean on Jesus' name." We believe there is no failure in God because we declare that on "Christ the Solid Rock we stand and all other ground is sinking sand!"

CHAPTER 9

GOD IS YOUR PEACE

"Let us draw near with a true heart in full assurance of faith, having our hearts sprinkled from an evil conscience and our bodies washed with pure water."

Hebrews 10:22 (NKJV)

A little boy visiting his grandparents was given his first slingshot. He practiced in the woods, but he could never hit his target. As he came back to grandma's backyard, he spied her pet duck. On an impulse he took aim and let it fly. The stone hit, and the duck fell dead. The boy panicked. Desperately, he hid the dead duck in the woodpile, only to look up and see his sister Sally watching. Sally had seen it all, but she said nothing.

After lunch that day, grandma said, " Sally lets wash the dishes." But Sally said, " Johnny told me he wanted to help in the kitchen today. Didn't you Johnny?" And then she whispered to Johnny, "remember the duck!" So, Johnny did the dishes.

Later grandpa asked if the children wanted to go fishing. Grandma said, "I'm sorry, but I need Sally to help me make supper." Sally smiled and said, "That's all taken care of. Johnny wants to do it." Again, she whispered to her brother, "remember the duck!" So, Johnny stayed while Sally went fishing.

After several days of Johnny doing both his chores and Sally's chores, he couldn't stand it any longer. He finally confessed to grandma that he'd killed the duck. "I know, Johnny," she said, while giving him a hug. "I was standing at the window and saw the whole thing. Because I love you, I already forgave you. But I wondered how long you would let Sally make you her slave."

This is what Satan does to us. He whispers to us, reminding us of our guilt. And this is what an evil conscience does to a person. This is the kind of guilty conscience described in Hebrews 10 - an evil conscience. And we've all experienced this at one time or another, and it's not a pleasant feeling at all.

However, this is not to suggest that our conscience itself is bad. Our conscience is a gift from God. Our conscience gives us the ability to see ourselves as someone else might see us. We want to keep our conscience sensitive so that we can hear the still, small voice of the Holy Spirit as He speaks. If we should lose this sensitivity, we then become vulnerable to our conscience being misled, and find ourselves being influenced by the opinions and views of other people instead of being responsive to the One who created us in His likeness. This is when the conscience becomes evil. Satan uses our conscience to tempt us to sin and to pierce us with guilt and shaming us when we fall. The Word of God itself calls us to keep our conscience clean. According to Acts 24:16 we are to "always strive to have a conscience without offense toward God and men."

An evil conscience is unable to discern between what is good and sinful, what is holy and what is wicked, what is true and what is a lie being told by Satan. In the end, an evil conscience fears death, for it overlooks God's grace and expects only bad things from God. Our guilt overwhelms us and our shame disgraces us, convincing us that we are not good enough. In the end, our evil conscience makes us a slave to the Law, much like Johnny was to his sister Sally.

In Hebrews 10 God invites us to come into His presence boldly, confident in knowing that He has made peace with us through the blood of Jesus Christ. Being at peace with God is an absolute great thing. But being at peace with yourself is an entirely different thing because an evil conscience can be a relentless voice deep within our soul, a voice often difficult to silence.

During Holy Week, celebrated yearly in the month of April, we commemorate the Passion of our Lord as he journeys to the cross. As the Word of God teaches, we will remember the evil conscience as it attacks and assaults Jesus' followers. However, it is here in this era that the word provided is with the defense we need against an evil conscience. By faith in Jesus, in His death for us and His mighty resurrection, we take up His shield of faith and overcome the assaults of Satan.

Hebrews 10:22 declares "Let us draw near (*accept this invitation to come in the presence of our Lord*) with a true heart in full assurance of faith (*completely believing and trusting in Him, with no reservations)* with our hearts sprinkled clean from an evil conscience *(cleansed by the blood of our Lord Jesus Christ)* and our bodies washed with pure water *(washed with the living water of the Holy Spirit that will never run dry)."*

When the high priest entered in behind the veil on the Day of Atonement, he did not go in lightly or carelessly. Instead, he took a ritual bath to cleanse himself. He would then carry in the blood of the sacrificial lamb and sprinkle it on the mercy seat on behalf of the people.

As God invites us to draw near, He reassures us that His cleansing goes much deeper than the outward bath. Jesus taught that what makes us unclean is not what lies on the surface but what comes out of our hearts. We are defiled by our sinful pride, our self-pity, our bitterness, our lust, our apathy on spiritual matters, and faithless fears. The only cleansing agent that can remove these stains is the blood of Jesus. We are edified through the Word of God, as Hebrews 9:13-14 declares "for if the blood of bulls and goats and the ashes of a heifer, sprinkling the unclean, sanctifies for the purifying of the flesh, how much more shall the blood of Christ, who through the eternal spirit offered Himself without spot to God, cleanse your conscience from dead works to serve the living God?"

So, why do you find it hard to make peace with yourself? Where is it that Satan assaults you with an evil conscience, whispering to you again and again, "remember the duck!" Use the Word of God as your shield, and there are three passages to consider as you go carry your weapon. Memorize them. Pray over them. Hold them before Satan and tell him,

"<u>I may not feel forgiven, but I trust God's Word, and I know that I know that I know that I am forgiven!</u>" Feelings may come and go. Feelings are often deceiving, but our shield is the Word of God and nothing else is worth believing.

The first passage is from 1 John 3:19-20: "by this we shall know that we are of the truth and reassure our heart before him; for whenever our heart condemns us, God is greater than our heart, and he knows everything." Again, God is greater than our heart. In other words, God is greater than your conscience. He knows the guilt and shame that haunts you. But set your heart at rest. Be at peace with yourself, not in your failed promises to do better, but in the Lord's promise that Jesus is full of forgiveness for you...**for you**...on the cross! It's only in Christ that we can find true peace and forgiveness. Forgiveness is a settled issue. Past, present, and future sin - all is washed away! The details of what we have done, why we did it, and how many times we did it are all irrelevant. Sin is sin; paid is paid; forgiven is forgiven; free is free. We can escape the gnawing accusations of our consciences by setting our minds on Jesus, fixed on the promises of The Master.

The second passage is from Psalm 103:11-12: "for as high as the heavens are above the earth, so great is His steadfast love toward those who fear Him; as far as the east is from the west, so far does He remove our transgressions from us." Aren't you glad that God didn't say "as far as north is from the south"? Fly north and the compass will eventually read south. But fly west and the compass will read west and fly east and the compass will continue to read east. East and west never meets. When God removes our sin in the blood of Jesus Christ, He will never recall it again. And neither should you.

There is no need to wallow in the past or to drudge it up. God has wiped your record clean!

The final passage in your arsenal is from John 8:36: "so if the Son sets you free, you will be free indeed." Will you really take Jesus at his Word? Will you really believe Him? What condemned Judas was not that he betrayed Jesus but that he did not believe Jesus. You see, Judas was an eyewitness when Jesus spoke His forgiving words to the adulterous woman. Jesus did not condemn her. He said, "go and sin no more." Judas was an eyewitness to Jesus' words of forgiveness when He told the paralytic man, "your sins are forgiven". And Judas was an eyewitness when Jesus spoke to the Samaritan woman, offering her grace from His living water, even in the midst of her sinful life. Yet when it came down to his own sin of betrayal, Judas could not believe that Jesus could pardon him. Judas could not make peace with himself, so much so that he ultimately committed suicide.

In contrast, look at the Apostle Peter. He denied knowing Jesus, denied having any type of relationship with Jesus, after just hours earlier boldly declaring that "I would even go to prison with you; I'll die with you." Peter was so ashamed of his actions that he ran away from the courtyard crying bitterly. But unlike Judas, Peter truly knew who Jesus was. Peter recognized Jesus' deity, His power, and His sonship in God by always addressing Him as Lord. Judas, on the other hand, would address Jesus as Rabbi. Although this is a title of honor and distinction, it does not recognize Jesus in His deity. Judas saw Jesus as merely a man. Peter had faith in the words of Jesus.

Proverbs 14:12 teaches us that "there is a way that seems right unto a man, but the end thereof are the ways of destruction." Judas thought his way was right, turning Jesus over to the priests in the temple, then getting all he could get from them, but in the end, he was destroyed. He could not live in peace with his actions, therefore, he couldn't accept the saving grace of Jesus Christ. But Peter also thought he was right in boldly confessing his allegiance to the Master, but when the rubber hit the road, his speech contradicted his actions. However, Peter accepted the saving grace and forgiveness of Jesus so they're relationship was restored.

Don't ever get to the point where you feel you could never have a restorative relationship with God the Father through His Son Jesus Christ. Just like the grandmother saw little Johnny kill her pet duck, God sees you. He sees the hurt, the shame, the embarrassment. But again, like grandma, He's waiting for you to come to Him, to be relieved of the anguish and agony of your wrong, and He will "give you peace that surpasses all understanding, which will guard your hearts and minds through Jesus", according to Philippians 4:7.

Isaiah 26:3 teaches us that God "will keep you in perfect peace, as your mind is stayed on Him, because you trust Him." And because you believe, although you don't see him, you can rejoice with joy unspeakable and full of glory. That's what 1 Peter 1:8 declares.

There is an old saying to "let your conscience be your guide". Is this good advice? It depends on how you train your conscience, your mind to guide you. The word conscience is spelled with two words: <u>con</u> and <u>science</u>. <u>Con</u> means *with*, and science is from the Latin word scire ("*she-ray*") which means *knowledge.* So, your mind is thinking with the knowledge you've been taught as your value system. In other words, your conscience will recall what you have accepted as right or wrong. Our conscience is trained by our parents, our schooling, our peers, and our circumstances in life. But know that in all of this, according to Paul in Romans 2:14-25, that God has put the basic principles, the basic knowledge of right and wrong in every person. Furthermore, Romans 1:20 teaches us that everyone is without excuse. Therefore, whenever a person goes against their God-given understanding of dishonoring God and his attributes, it is sin. When you understand that God is loving and kind and compassionate and forgiving and the God of peace, why do you choose to follow lying spirits and teachings that come from demons, teachers who are hypocrites and liars? In doing so you've allowed sin to sear your conscience.

When Jesus spoke the words on the cross "it is finished", that phrase meant "paid in full". No one can hold any debt against you any longer because the debt has been fully paid on your behalf. The requirements to receive the full payment was met. The requirement is to acknowledge Jesus Christ as the Son of God. The requirement is to accept that He died on Calvary's cross for your sins. The requirement is to believe that He rose from the dead, was resurrected with all power in his hand. The requirement is to accept the free gift of salvation today. And with that free gift of salvation, you will receive the peace that you've been looking for everywhere else. With that free gift of salvation, you will receive forgiveness from all your sins, past, present, and future. With that free gift of salvation, you will be set free from all the guilt and shame and condemnation that you've placed on yourself far too long. Let God be your peace and you will walk in freedom.

CHAPTER 10
REDEEM THE TIME WITH GOD

¹"Lord, You have been our dwelling place in all generations. ²Before the mountains were brought forth, or ever You had formed the earth and the world, even from everlasting to everlasting, You are God. ³You turn man to destruction, and say, "Return, O children of men." ⁴For a thousand years in Your sight are like yesterday when it is past, and like a watch in the night. ⁵You carry them away like a flood; they are like a sleep. In the morning they are like grass which grows up: ⁶In the morning it flourishes and grows up; in the evening it is cut down and withers. ⁷For we have been consumed by Your anger, and by Your wrath we are terrified. ⁸You have set our iniquities before You, our secret sins in the light of Your countenance. ⁹For all our days have passed away in Your wrath; We finish our years like a sigh. ¹⁰The days of our lives are seventy years; And if by reason of strength they are eighty years, yet their boast is only labor and sorrow; For it is soon cut off, and we fly away. ¹¹Who knows the power of Your anger? For as the fear of You, so is Your wrath. ¹²So teach us to number our days, that we may gain a heart of wisdom."

Psalms 90:1-12 NKJV

When we were children, we thought we had all the time in the world to do whatever we wanted to do. When I was a child, we played outside all day. Sure, we would come in the house to have lunch and dinner, and whatever our mother would have us to do, but as soon as we were able to do so, we'd run back outside to run, jump, flip, and have all kinds of fun. We'd lay on the ground and look up at the clouds in the sky and imagine the shapes to be certain images - perhaps a dog, a man's face, a horse, or even pink cotton candy. We'd sing the nursery rhyme with our friends of what we might want to be when we grow up: rich man, poor man, beggar man, thief, a doctor, a lawyer or an Indian chief. We believed that time was on our side.

But as we became adults and began to experience life, we realized that time was not on our side. Life has shown us things we never dreamed of experiencing: illegal drugs infiltrating society; communicable diseases spreading; wars ravaging inside and outside of our country; innocent children being killed or even sold into sex trafficking; deadly gangs developing across this country; and lives ending unexpectedly in just the blink of an eye. We realize as adults that childish games have to end and that we must concentrate on surviving in this world in which we live. We realize that some of our dreams had to either be put on hold or no longer exist so that we could take care of more urgent family needs, or we just didn't have the resources to make it come to fruition.

There is a time in all our lives when we must face the ultimate reality that our lives exist for a fleeting moment. We must see from God's perspective, that we are but dust from the earth and to the dust we will return. James 4:14 says that we don't know what tomorrow will bring, and that our life is a mist which appears for a little while then vanishes, like a morning fog that appears for a while but then disappears. So as children of God, we must not be foolish like the world and live a life of folly. We must not live like tomorrow is promised.

I remember when my sister came home from school one day to declare a revelation that her second grade teacher gave the class, which was that "tomorrow never comes". The idea is that tomorrow is not definitive. We can speak of yesterday because there is a date attached to it. But we can't attach a definitive date to tomorrow because there will always be tomorrow. Remember when you were a child, you'd ask your parents for something to have or something to do and their answer would be <u>tomorrow?</u> You'd go back and ask the same question and you'd get the same answer: <u>tomorrow</u>. But today is definitive. Today is Thursday, February 16, 2023. Today is now. Today is present tense. That's why the scripture urgently pleads with the unbeliever in 2 Corinthians 6:2 that "now is the accepted time; behold, now (<u>today</u>) is the day of salvation." Also, the plea goes out in Hebrews 3:15, "<u>today</u>, if you hear his voice, do not harden your hearts as you did in the rebellion."

We should live our lives as if today is the last day of our lives. As Psalm 90:4 points out, and also in 2 Peter 3:8, the Word of the Lord teaches us not to forget that "a day to the Lord is like a thousand years and a thousand years is like a day". We must be conscious of the fact that at any given time Christ will return, and we don't want to be caught with our work undone. James 4:15 instructs us that we should say "if the Lord wills, I will do this or that". We don't boast in our own arrogance that we have all the time. That is evil. We need to recognize that it is God who has a set time for everyone's life. He is not working according to our timetable.

Psalm 90 is considered to be a prayer of Moses, the great leader of Israel, and written during their years in the wilderness on the way to Canaan. As the Word of God teaches, the Israelites had an extremely difficult period of time as slaves in the land of Egypt, until God assigned Moses the task of leading the Israelites out of Egypt's bondage and into freedom. The scriptures let us know of their excitement as well as their fear of leaving familiar territory, although conditions were not favorable to them. They were excited about their new lives in a land that God had prepared for them. They were excited because a new beginning was awaiting them. They were excited because they felt like they were finally being rescued from their misery. But they also feared the unknown. They feared of how they would be taken care of along the dry and deserted journey. They feared that they would die in the middle of nowhere and that buzzards would eat their carcasses.

They quickly forgot about the God who was Elohim, the Almighty God, who was with their forefathers, Abraham, Isaac, and Jacob. They forgot that God was God before the mountains were brought forth, and that He is from everlasting to everlasting, and that He can do all things but fail. But the question is asked: are we not like the Israelites? Do we forget the power of God when our plans go awry? Do we feel like all hope is lost when life is constantly giving us sour lemons? Do we forget that God is sovereign and that His plans and purposes are perfect? Do we forget that time is a gift from

God and that His children have been charged to redeem the time?

Ephesians 5:15-16 teaches us that "we should walk circumspectly, and not as fools, but as the wise, redeeming the time, because the days are evil". In other words, we need to be very mindful and careful how we conduct our lives. We don't live our lives like we have all the time in the world, to put off those things we have been tasked to do. We should not procrastinate in completing those assignments that God has purposed us to do. This is what the fools of the world, the unbelievers of Jesus Christ do. They drink and be merry, thinking that tomorrow they'll have another chance to do this or that. But "the iniquities of the world are ever before the Sovereign God", as pointed out in Psalm 90:8. Even the secret sins, that we think we can keep to ourselves. God sees them all.

Let's not forget about the parable that Jesus told of the rich man in Luke 12:16 - 21. Here we have a man who was extremely wealthy from having a farm that produced many fine crops. This is an example not only of a man who was so focused on his material wealth, but it's also the story of a man who did not have the sense to do good with what he was blessed with. He was blessed with so much crop that he chose to build bigger barns to store his goods. He chose to tear down what he already had, the smaller barns that already stored his goods. This man didn't have the mind to use his time wisely to bless others with his wealth. This man did not have the mind to share his many crops with neighbors who may have been less fortunate than him. This man chose not to use his time wisely to consult God on how to use his overabundance of goods for kingdom building. This man chose to sit back, eat, drink, and be merry, for he felt that he had all he needed for years to come. But God called his name and the rich man died on the very night he was making these declarations to himself. After all that, he was unable to use any of the things he collected for himself. This is an example of a fool, for verse 21 of Luke 12 says that "a fool is a person who stores up earthly wealth and not have a rich relationship with God."

So that we don't fall into the same fatal position as the foolish rich man, let us try to be attentive to the following three points:

Point #1 - Reflect On The Brevity/The Shortness Of Life

I still remember having my 6th grade teacher tell me that the older we get, that time will fly by faster than when we were children. And I found this to be so true. As children, we thought it took forever for Christmas to come each year. Now, we celebrate Christmas one day and it seems like we're celebrating it again after a few short months. One day we are celebrating the birth of a child. What seems like a few short years later, we look up and then we're celebrating that child's high school graduation. In Psalm 90:12 Moses is praying that we would be taught to number our days carefully, so that we may develop wisdom in our hearts. In other words, we need to consider the shortness of our lives and the certainty of death, so that we may devote ourselves to fervently studying the Word of God and practice true wisdom.

Point #2 - Realize The Uncertainty Of Tomorrow

We certainly should save, work, plan, and prepare for life's issues and circumstances well into the future. However, we must realize that there is not a guarantee to see the future. There is not even a guarantee to see tomorrow. I mentioned James 4 earlier, but notice the entire words that James spoke to the Jewish Christians who were scattered throughout other countries from Jerusalem due to persecution for their belief in Jesus Christ: James 4:13-16 from the New Living Translation reads, "you who say, "Today or tomorrow we are going to a certain town and will stay there a year. We will do business there and make a profit." How do you know what your life will be like tomorrow? Your life is like the morning fog. It's here a little while, then it's gone. What you ought to say is, "If the Lord wants us to, we will live and do this or that." Otherwise, you are boasting about your own pretentious plans, and all such boasting is evil." Life is short no matter how long you live. Don't be deceived into thinking that you will have lots of time to live for Christ, to enjoy your loved ones, or to do what you know you should do. You should live for God today.

Point #3 - Remember That Time Is Your Most Precious Possession

Contrary to popular belief, money is not your most precious possession. Time is your most precious possession. And we tend to throw away our time in some of the most non-beneficial ways: scrolling through social media; flicking through over 100 television channels; idle chatter; and just plain old procrastination.

Donald Whitney, an author and professor at the Southern Baptist Theological Seminary in Louisville, Kentucky, said that "if people threw away their money as thoughtlessly as they throw away their time, we would think them to be insane. Yet time is infinitely more precious than money because money cannot buy time." We should consider this for the kingdom work of God. Our allotment of time is a special gift from God, and we are charged to be good stewards of it for spreading the gospel of Jesus Christ.

So, you may ask, how can I redeem the time that God has granted unto me? Well, first our time should glorify God because we want to reflect all that He is, in whatever we do. In Matthew 6:33 Jesus teaches that we should "seek first the kingdom of God and his righteousness." When you follow this command, you are putting God first in your life, filling your thoughts with His desires, taking His character as a pattern for your life, and serve and obey Him in everything.

Psalm 63:1 reads "oh God, You are my God, earnestly I seek you. My soul thirsts for you. My flesh faints for you, as in a dry and weary land where there is no water." With this psalm in mind, ask yourself, do you prioritize your faith? Do you make time for daily bible study and prayer? Do you engage in family prayer time and worship? Do you plan a specific time or times to be alone with God?

You can redeem the time by referring to what the Word of the Lord said to Zerubbabel, the Old Testament governor of Jerusalem, as written in Zechariah 4:6 "not by might, nor by power, but by my Spirit." Zerubbabel had the awesome task of leading the exiled children of God from Babylon to Jerusalem. These people were discouraged, having been under Babylonian rule for 70 years, and now that it's time to return home, what was there to return to? Their land was destroyed. There was no life and seemingly no hope to be seen anywhere.

When you feel discouraged and hopeless in your situation, know that you can redeem the time by continuing to work for the kingdom of God in spite of your feelings. You can redeem the time by recognizing that the Spirit of God that lives within you, will enable you, by His power, to do what is necessary to get the assigned tasks accomplished.

You can redeem the time by following 2 Chronicles 20:20, words that King Jehoshaphat spoke to all the people of Judah before they began their battle against the men of Ammon, Moab, and Mt. Seir. He gave them words of encouragement that we can hold on to today as well, and that is to "believe in the LORD your God, and you shall be established". God is the same yesterday, today, and forever. He has and always will be faithful to you. We can have faith in the God who continues to establish your feet, give you a permanent relationship, one that will never change, and He will uphold you with His righteous right hand. King Jehoshaphat also advised the people of Judah to have faith in the prophets, those men who were God appointed messengers, and in doing so, they would be successful.

There is so much going on in his world today that it behooves the people of God to be very aware that there is plenty of work to be done before the Lord returns. The days are evil, which is why we need to stand up for righteousness in the face of evil. We need to speak truth in the midst of lies.

We need to present our bodies as a living sacrifice. God does not require the blood of goats or lamb. The blood of Jesus Christ satisfied the law for atonement on Calvary's cross. In the book of 1 Samuel, chapter 15, the prophet Samuel asked the question to King Saul after he did evil in the eyes of God by taking the spoils of the enemy, after God gave him direct instructions to destroy everything: "Does the Lord take pleasure in burnt offerings and sacrifices as much as he does in obedience? Certainly, obedience is better than sacrifice; paying attention is better than the fat of rams."

We can redeem the time by being obedient to the Word of the Lord: go where He says go; move when He says move; be quiet when He says be quiet. We can redeem the time by following Galatians 5:24, which is to "crucify the flesh with its passions and desires". We belong to Jesus Christ and are to be led by His Spirit and not by the spirit of this world.

We can redeem the time by following Paul's teachings in 1 Corinthians 2:1-4, where he explains to the church in Corinth that he did not come to preach or proclaim the Word of God by using big words or of his own intellect or his opinions, but he made up his mind that he was coming to preach only Jesus the Christ and His death on the cross. He went on explain that he was coming to speak not from his wisdom but only by the power of the Spirit of God.

We can redeem the time by following David's words in Psalm 101:2-3, New Living Translation: "I will be careful to live a blameless life— when will you come to help me? I will lead a life of integrity in my own home. I will refuse to look at anything vile and vulgar. I hate all who deal crookedly; I will have nothing to do with them." What are your standards in your own home? What example are you setting before your children? Are you wasting time looking at nonsense television shows and engaging in gossip conversations? Are you involved with people who practice evil and wickedness, who are against the standards of God and His righteousness? David said he will be careful to live a wholesome life, one of integrity, before God. He said he hates anyone who has anything to do with crookedness and wickedness and evil schemes against the things of God and he will have nothing to do with them. Are you in agreement with David's words? Are you mindful of your time in this regard? This can only be done by the Spirit of God, just as David asked for His help.

Ephesians 5:16 lets us know why we should redeem the time, or in other words, why we should be mindful of the use of our time. The reason is because the days of this world we live in are evil, they are wicked, profoundly immoral. We don't need to waste our God-given time on the flirtations and deceptions of this world when enough time has been given to accomplish the purposes which God has designed for each of us. Jesus taught in Matthew 28:18 that we have been empowered by the Spirit of God in heaven and on earth to follow His command in Matthew 28:19, and that is to "go and make disciples of all the nations, baptizing them in the name of the Father and of the Son and of the Holy Spirit". The people of God have a responsibility to proclaim, to declare, the good news of Jesus Christ. We are to preach, and I don't mean the position of a preacher in a pulpit, or a pastor of a church, or reverend/minister in front of your name. God spoke His Word to Isaiah in 58:1, that is relevant for every believer today, and He said, " cry loud, spare not, lift up your voice like a trumpet; tell my people of their transgressions and the house of Jacob of their sins."

And in Matthew 28:20 we're charged to go even further in our kingdom work and that is to teach these new disciples, these new converts, to observe all the things that Jesus has commanded us. Teach, as in explain, expound, on the information that was presented to you, which caused you to surrender your life to Christ and make Him your Savior. And while we're doing this work, we can be assured that Jesus is with us always, even to the end of the age.

We're not children anymore, thinking that we have all the time in the world to play around and not follow Jesus. However, there is something we can do that some little children do today. They play a game called "Follow the Leader". Whatever the leader does that's what the child or children would do. If the leader hopped on one foot, the children would hop on one foot. If the leader would touch his nose, they would do the same and touch their nose. If the leader did Jumping Jacks nonstop for 10 minutes, the children would do the same, or at least attempt to do so. We should have the same mindset as in the game "Follow the Leader". Our Leader is Jesus Christ and we as Christians, disciples of Jesus Christ, are to follow Him wherever He leads.

Time is a valuable gift from God, that should be used wisely for kingdom building. So, remember that your days are numbered, and don't waste this valuable gift when you can redeem the time today.

CHAPTER 11
GOD IS THE KEY TO YOUR FUTURE

¹³"When Jesus came into the region of Caesarea Philippi, He asked His disciples, saying, "Who do men say that I, the Son of Man, am?" ¹⁴ So they said, "Some say John the Baptist, some Elijah, and others Jeremiah or one of the prophets." ¹⁵ He said to them, "But who do you say that I am?" ¹⁶ Simon Peter answered and said, "You are the Christ, the Son of the living God." ¹⁷ Jesus answered and said to him, "Blessed are you, Simon Bar-Jonah, for flesh and blood has not revealed this to you, but My Father who is in heaven. ¹⁸ And I also say to you that you are Peter, and on this rock I will build My church, and the gates of Hades shall not [a]prevail against it. ¹⁹ And I will give you the keys of the kingdom of heaven, and whatever you bind on earth [b]will be bound in heaven, and whatever you loose on earth will be loosed in heaven."

Matthew 16:13-19 (NKJV)

I have several sets of keys that I use for various reasons. I have a set of keys that give me access to my mother's house: keys to the front door, which gains me entrance to the front of the house, and keys to what we call the den door, which gains me entrance directly into the den of the house. I have keys to the three cars at my house, a Kia Optima, a Ford Edge, and a Toyota Prius. Without using the correct key, I won't have access to drive any of the cars whenever I or my husband wants to do so. And then of course I have keys to my house, to the front door, the back door and the storm doors at each entrance. Without my keys, there is no way I could get into my house, unless I break a window to gain access.

I would think it strange to have a bunch of keys in one's possession, just for looks only, and not use them for the purpose in which they were given. I don't understand why anyone would want to have a bunch of jingle and jangling keys on them, other than wanting to sound like Santa Clause coming to town at Christmas. As a child of God, you should know that you have every right to use your keys to the kingdom of God and you have been given the authority to use your keys for the kingdom of God.

At the beginning of chapter 16 in Matthew we see that Jesus encountered the religious leaders, the Pharisees and Sadducees. To give a little background information, these two groups of men really didn't like each other very much, nor did they trust each other, although they are supposedly God-fearing Jewish men. They didn't see eye to eye on scriptural understandings.

The Pharisees believed in the Old Testament laws, but they also included their own religious traditions, believing they were of equal authority, and by following them it would gain them entrance to live with God. The Sadducees believed only in the written words of the Hebrew Scriptures, that is the Books of Moses. If they couldn't find the command in the Hebrew Scriptures, they dismissed it as manmade.

The Pharisees believed in angels and the resurrection. The Sadducees did not. They followed the teachings in Genesis through Deuteronomy, or The Mosaic Law. They also believed in Levitical purity, all of which did not explicitly teach on the resurrection.

The Pharisees were not a political party and were prepared to live under any government that would leave them alone to practice their religion any way they wanted to. The Sadducees were aristocrats and collaborated with the Roman government to keep their wealth and power.

Although these two groups of men were on polar opposites of the religious spectrum, they both were so opposed to the person of Jesus and who He claimed to be, that they swallowed their pride enough to come together, against Jesus, to find fault with Him, because He challenged their prideful attitudes and dishonorable motives. Jesus was a serious threat to each of them.

In the discourse of the scripture in Matthew 16, these religious leaders wanted Jesus to show them a sign, a miracle from heaven. Of course, Jesus knew the intention of these men's hearts and knew there was no sincerity of actually getting to know Him. Up to his point He had already performed so many miracles which they chose not to believe. They saw Him feed more than 5,000 people with five loaves of bread and two fish. They saw Him heal the sick, open the eyes of the blind, unstop deaf ears, raise people from the dead. Their belief was that any signs or miracles done on the earth could be a counterfeit from Satan, but signs from heaven, coming down from the sky, or in the sky, were from God, as we see in Matthew 16:1, where they ask Jesus specifically for a sign from heaven. They perhaps were looking for Jesus to call down fire from heaven, and the Pharisees probably wanted it to fall on a Roman legion. But they all were fakes. The Pharisees and Sadducees had no true desire to know Jesus as the Messiah. They had ulterior motives. Both the Pharisees and Sadducees had a great number of people following them. The Pharisees had the following and respect of the common working people, while the Sadducees were popular among the Roman government. They both were out for personal gain, not for the good of the people.

Just as the disciples understood Jesus tell them in Matthew 16:12 to beware of the doctrine of the Pharisees and Sadducees, believers also need to be careful who they allow to speak in their ears and who they choose to follow in the name of Jesus. There are plenty of charlatans today who sound good and look good, but they are no good! Remember, that just because someone can quote scriptures at the drop of a hat doesn't mean they are for the cause of Christ. Satan knows how to manipulate the Word of God to make it sound accurate and appealing to your current situation. Don't forget how he tried to deceive Jesus in the wilderness even with the holy scriptures, thinking he can use the Sword of the Spirit for his personal gain. If you didn't know any better, you'd think Satan was a card-carrying member of "the worldwide bible scholars club"! Satan is so cunning that he knows how to transform himself into an angel of light, as we're taught by the Apostle Paul in 2 Corinthians 11:14, when in fact he is the prince of darkness, which is what Paul called him in Colossians 1:13.

The Pharisees and Sadducees were no different then, than many people of this world today. As 2 Timothy 3:5 puts it, "they act as if they are religious, but they will reject the power that could make them godly." The King James Version says it this way: "having a form of godliness but denying the power thereof; from such turn away".

We all know these people, who know how to look religious by going to church with their bible in hand, by wearing the proper attire, and by knowing Christian doctrine. They know how to use Christian cliches and follow Christian traditions. They look good, really good, but if their inner man does not truly believe, love, and worship Jesus Christ, the outer man's appearance is meaningless. People of God, use your keys to unlock and renew your mind when Satan comes to attack, cunningly using God's Word against you. You hit him back with the word from 1 John 4:4, "I am a child of God and am an overcomer because Jesus, who is in me, is greater than he, the devil, who is in the world". You also tell him that Luke 10:19 declares that "Jesus has given me authority to trample on serpents and scorpions, and over all the power of the enemy, and nothing shall by any means harm me".

Jesus called the religious leaders "a wicked and adulterous generation". He called them men who were evil and idolatrous, loving themselves and their agenda instead of loving the Messiah standing before them. Jesus knew that miracles never convinced anyone who was already skeptical. Do you expect Jesus to prove Himself to you with some sort of sign before you surrender your life to Him? Are you like the chief priests and the scribes, who were at the crucifixion of Jesus, mocking him, saying that if he is truly the King of Israel and the Son of God, if He would come down from the cross, then they'd believe him? Jesus told Thomas in John 10:29 "blessed are those who have not seen and have believed".

There are miracles recorded in the Old and New Testaments, over 2,000 years of church history, and the witness of thousands, and there will still be people who won't believe, just like the Pharisees and Sadducees. Jesus said in Matthew 16:4 the only sign that He will give people to believe is likened to that of the prophet Jonah. Jonah was in the belly of the great fish for three days and three nights. He sacrificed himself so that others could be saved. He disappeared from all human sight for three days and three nights. He came back from what seemed like the dead after three days and three nights, and then he preached repentance to a wicked and evil nation. So, Jesus did as well. But He is greater than Jonah. He did rise from the dead, after three days and three nights, and His resurrection proved that He is the Messiah, that He is the Son of the living God. He showed Himself to be far more superior than all the ancient prophets and messengers of God.

Use your keys to unlock and renew your mind when doubters and haters come asking why you believe in a God that cannot be seen with the naked eye. You boldly declare John 3:16, making it personal, that "God loved me so greatly and considered me to be a precious treasure to Him that He gave up His one and only Son for me, and that if I would just believe and trust Him as my Savior, then I will not perish but instead would have eternal life in heaven." You can also repeat what Paul said in Galatians 2:20: "I have been crucified with Christ; it is no longer I but Christ who lives in me; and the life which I now live in the flesh I live by faith in the Son of God, who loved me and gave Himself for me".

Who is Jesus to you? What does He mean to you? How important is your relationship with Him? Is He just a good preacher or a good teacher, sharing His knowledge of a world that is completely incomprehensible to you? Is He a fortune teller, being able to tell of events that may happen in your life? Is He a rabble-rouser, someone who wants to overturn and upset the normalcies of your life? Or is He to you what Simon Peter declared, that He is the Christ, the Anointed One, the Messiah, the Son of the living God? Use your keys to unlock the false narratives of who Jesus is. He is the shining light in a dark world. He is manna, the bread from heaven. He is the living water in a dry and thirsty land. He is a covenant keeper. He is the seed of David, the Lion of Judah, the King of Kings, the reigning King forevermore!

Don't you know that once you use your keys and unlock the door to your God ordained destiny that a shift will occur in the atmosphere? That's what's supposed to happen! Nothing is supposed to remain the same! Why do you think people say to you when they meet you, "there's something different about you. I can't put my finger on it but there's an aura about you"? It's a God-thing and many people won't understand, but you do because you know the power of having the keys to the kingdom. You walk in a room and heads turn. You speak and people want to hear the wisdom of God coming from your mouth. They want to talk to you because you've learned to listen with the Spirit of God leading you before you respond to their inquiries. All of this is because you have been delivered from the power of darkness and have been given access to the kingdom of the Lord Jesus Christ. You can see the kingdom clearly now because you have kingdom vision. You can hear the Spirit of God sharper now because you have kingdom ears. You walk in confidence now, because you walk by faith and not by sight.

There is power with kingdom keys and Jesus is the door to gain access to that power. He is the door to new possibilities and opportunities. He is the door to a new image, as you can be transformed into the image of the Lord from glory to glory. He is the door to a new way of thinking, that no matter what you've done BC (before Christ), there is now no condemnation to those who are in Christ Jesus, for He has already freed you from the law of sin and death. All you have to do is use your keys to free your mind from Satan's lies. Jesus is the door to deliverance, as you can escape the corruption of this world if you would just use your keys to gain access to the great and precious promises that await those who are partakers of His divine nature. Jesus is the door to your kingdom authority, so use your keys to take authority over Satan, and bind the works of the enemy, over every plan he wants to bring to prevent you from gaining access to your kingdom rights and privileges, as he ultimately wants to destroy your life.

Remember that the weapons of your warfare are not carnal, but they are mighty through God, by the pulling down of strongholds. Use your keys to loosen the powers, or to permit the powers, of heaven in your life, and gain you access to abundance and not lack. Use your keys for you to gain access to wealth and not poverty. Use your keys for you to gain access to freedom and not be in captivity. Use your keys for you to gain access to safety and protection, and not wandering and loneliness. Use your keys for you to gain access to joy and gladness, and not depression and oppression. Use your keys for you to gain access to peace of mind and not turmoil of the heart. Use your keys for you to gain access to love one another and not keep bitterness intact.

People of God need to use their keys to preach/to declare/to evangelize the gospel of Jesus Christ, opening the kingdom of heaven to all believers and carry out the will of the Father. It is the ministry of the church, the bride of Christ, to loosen people from the power of Satan and from the chains and bondage of sin, and to bind the demonic forces set against God and His people. But the people will never hear the Good News of the Gospel unless those who have the keys don't open their mouth and proclaim the message of Jesus Christ to a dying world.

I mentioned earlier in this chapter that without my keys, there is no way I could get into my house, unless I break a window to gain access. If you have established a relationship with Jesus Christ, there is no need for you to break into anything to gain access to the kingdom of God and everything He has already given you access to. If you have established a relationship with Jesus Christ, you are a joint heir with Him, meaning you are seated in the heavenly places with the Father and have already been given the same access as the Son.

However, if you have not established a relationship with Jesus Christ and you try to gain access to the kingdom of God some other way, whether by sneaking in, or climbing in, or going around to get in, then the scripture in John 10:1 calls you a thief and a robber. You're a thief because you think you can gain access to the kingdom by some secret way that's not known to everyone else, and you're a robber because you won't have any hesitancy to commit violence or bloodshed to get what you want.

I want to conclude this chapter with the last three words reported to have been spoken out of the mouth of the late civil rights leader Medger Evers as he was being transported to the University of Mississippi Medical Center, after being shot by white supremacist Byron De La Beckwith Jr in 1963. Those last three words were "turn me loose". After all the deplorable experiences he went through in his lifetime, all the Jim Crow laws, all the hatred, having been denied entrance to University of Mississippi, all the bomb threats, and even unsuccessful attempts to his home, he was now free. I can't help but think that for a brief moment he had the thought that he no longer had to suffer the evils of this present world. For a brief moment, perhaps he had the thought that victory is now his because he is loosed from Satan's wickedness. For him to utter the last words "turn me loose" was as if he would say, "I've used the keys given to me; I've fought a good fight, I've run the race set before me, and in spite of all the wrongs done to me, I am no longer bound but now I am free indeed."

So, let us use our keys to be turned loose from every demonic influence that has infiltrated our lives. Bind that spirit of unforgiveness and use your keys to be loosed to receive the spirit of forgiveness from heaven. Bind that spirit of pride and use your keys to be loosed to receive the spirit of humility from heaven. Bind that spirit of jealousy and resentment and use your keys to receive the spirit of kindness and contentment. Bind that spirit of hatred and use your keys to be loosed to receive the love of God through his Son Jesus Christ.

You can be loosed and receive access to the things of God only by receiving the keys to the kingdom, and the keys to the kingdom are only received by having a relationship with Jesus Christ. There is no other way, for He is the only way, the only truth, and the only life. No one comes to the Father but by Him. If you already have the keys to the kingdom, use them with the authority and power in which they've been given. Don't hold on to something this valuable and not take advantage of its purpose.

If you don't have the keys to the kingdom, it's not too late to receive them now. Accept Jesus Christ as your Savior today and all the advantages, privileges, and rights to a kingdom kid, a child of God, will belong to you today.

CHAPTER 12

GOD IS THE HOUSE IN WHICH TO ABIDE

43"When an unclean spirit goes out of a man, he goes through dry places, seeking rest, and finds none. 44Then he says, 'I will return to my house from which I came.' And when he comes, he finds it empty, swept, and put in order. 45Then he goes and takes with him seven other spirits more wicked than himself, and they enter and dwell there; and the last state of that man is worse than the first. So shall it also be with this wicked generation."

Matthew 12:43-45 (NKJV)

I enjoy watching the cable TV station HGTV. I get some of my decorating ideas from some of the featured shows. I like watching "House Hunters" and "My Lottery Dream House", where people from different states in this country search for their new home.

I particularly like to look at the shows that take old, run-down houses, refurbish them, renovate them, remodel them, and make them into a completely new house. Then they put in fresh, new furnishings to give it a completely new look. "Flip or Flop" is a show that specializes in this work. Some of the houses shown were bought at auction, some at a very low price, to be completely refurbished. Some of these houses are terribly run down, with broken windows, rotten floorboards, leaky roofs, rat and roach infested, some have an awful odor inside. But when the makeover is complete, there is very little sign of what the house used to look like.

And then there is the show "Fixer Upper" where there are some houses that have been kept in families for generations, that need repairing here and there, some remodeling, and some updates.

When we first come to Christ, we are a mess, like a lot of the houses shown on "Flip or Flop" and "Fixer Upper". Isaiah 64:6 says that "all our righteousness is as filthy rags". So, a complete renovation needs to take place in our soul. There is old, raggedy stuff that needs to be removed and thrown away. When you want to renovate your house, you don't want to keep the clutter you had before. Even if you had some good memorabilia, if it doesn't fit in with your current lifestyle, then it needs to be discarded. For instance, the disco ball was popular in the 1970s and it was cool to have one displayed in your house at that time, but it's now time to let it go. Or the lava lamp that had the slow-motion gook moving around in a glass, it's time to let that go too. When we renovate and remodel, we don't keep what's old. We make room for the new.

In the above-mentioned scripture reference in Matthew 12:43-45, there is a renovation that was taking place, but it wasn't complete. From the outside it appeared that everything was clean and spotless. The appearance was that the owner had everything well put together. But when you looked more closely everything wasn't as clean and put together as it appeared. The owner neglected a very important detail in his cleaning. Let's look at this scripture text more closely.

First let's be clear. Your spirit/your life is the house that the enemy is looking to reside in. When you hear someone say, "I am very spiritual", I would agree with that statement. Every person is spiritual because every person has a spirit that resides in them. The question is whether the person is filled with the Holy Spirit of God or is the person filled with the demonic spirit of Satan and his cohorts. The scripture distinctly lets us know how to tell one spirit from another, and we will discuss that more in a moment.

We see in the scripture text a person who wanted to change his house/his life. Perhaps he no longer wanted to live the fast life he was accustomed to. Perhaps he wanted to quit going out to clubs. Perhaps he wanted to quit sleeping around with various women and men. Perhaps he wanted to quit doing drugs. Perhaps he wanted to quit using profanity as part of his everyday vocabulary. Perhaps he wanted new friends and didn't want to hang out with the gang bangers any longer. Perhaps he didn't want to hang out with the depressed and oppressed groups any longer. He just wanted a complete change in his life. So, he decided to start by cleaning up his house.

He had the right idea and was headed on the right road. He went into every nook and cranny of his life and cleaned up everything that was contrary to his present desires. He no longer had the desire to go to the places he used to hang out.

He no longer had the desire to use the same vocabulary he had before. He no longer had the desire to hang out with people he used to call his road dogs. He even found new friends that he truly enjoyed being with. Ephesians 5:5 teaches "no whoremonger, nor unclean person, nor covetous man, who is an idolater, has any inheritance in the kingdom of Christ and of God". He was good. Everything was cool. Everything was fine. Everything was cleaned up very well. But something happened unexpectedly.

This person began to have feelings that he hadn't had in quite a long time. He began to have feelings of depression, so much so that suicidal thoughts began to occupy his mind. He never had thoughts of suicide before but now here they are. He couldn't see clearly any longer. He became discombobulated and confused in his mind. He became tired, broken, and run down. He kept hearing voices that he never heard before, telling him to do things to harm himself and others. So, he began to medicate himself with prescribed pills, but they didn't seem to turn things around for him. Then he began to medicate himself with unprescribed pills, gotten from the corner drug dealer. He turned to anything that would turn off the voices in his head, from pills, to dope, to alcohol, but nothing helped. This was all new to him.

He is soon to discover what John 10:10 really means, that "the thief comes not, but for to steal, and to kill, and to destroy". All that he did to clean his house, his spirit man, his life, was now being destroyed by the enemy. Remember, although his house was cleansed, it was also empty. The man failed to replace it with new things that would benefit his life. So, what happened? The enemy saw that the house was clean, and he also saw that it was empty. Since he left to find a new place to reside and he didn't find one, he decided to go back home, and he brought his many friends with him. There's no place like home, right? But when he brought his friends with him this caused the man to experience behaviors that he never had before. Now what happened to this man? Why couldn't he be left alone to enjoy his newly renovated house? Why couldn't he enjoy his newly cleansed life?

People of God need to be aware of the lesson in Mark 2:22, where the Word of the Lord speaks "no one pours new wine into old wineskins, or else the new wine will burst the wineskins, the wine is spilled, and the wineskins are ruined. But new wine must be put into new wineskins." This man was trying to put a new thing into an old house. He wanted the Spirit of God (that new thing) but he did not clean his old house to rid it completely of the old thing (the old man). It was good that he was able to remove the old habits, the old talk, and the old friends, but what did he put in place of those old things? <u>NOTHING</u>.

To explain Mark 2:22 a little further, in the fermentation process, new wine will burst old bottles made of wineskins that are not strong enough to resist the strength of the fermenting fluid because it swells during the process. So, the bottles of old wineskins will burst, wasting the bottles and wine. Therefore, new wine must be poured into bottles made from fresh, new wineskins, which are tough and strengthened to withstand the fermentation of the new wine. Jesus is teaching that it is detrimental to anyone who tries to mix and mingle together the new nature of man, found in the Spirit of God, with the old nature of the sinful man.

When one comes to Christ, after denying the old sinful nature, he must submit himself to the nature and standards of Jesus Christ. The man in Matthew 12:43-45 is an illustration of someone who should have immediately replaced the cleaned-up old house/his old nature, with the pure, holy, perfect nature of the Holy Spirit. He neglected to do that. He was like the HGTV show "<u>Fixer Upper</u>", where he acknowledged that a new work needed to be done, remodeling was required, and he was willing to do the work, but he was also like the other HGTV show "<u>Flip or Flop</u>". An attempt to flip his house was made, but it ended up being a flop because he did not complete the process of the cleansing. He was in his right mind as long as the old nature/the unclean spirit was gone, and the house was swept clean. Everything was in order as long as the unclean spirit wasn't there. But again, the man failed to bring into the house that which was good. He left the house in the same common routine of his former life. Although he stopped his old practices, he took no thought of completely remodeling and refurbishing the house to match that of the King's house. If he did, that would have prevented the enemy from coming back with his many friends. The enemy was so bold to announce that he was going to return to "my house", which meant he had ownership, he had possession of the man.

Well, you may ask, what can I do to ensure that the new nature of the Holy Spirit is placed in my house, in my life, after it's been cleansed of the enemy? In other words, what can I do once I have been delivered from whatever it is that has separated me from God? How can I walk in my deliverance?

First, James 4:7-8 teaches "Therefore submit to God. Resist the devil and he will flee from you. Draw near to God and He will draw near to you. Cleanse your hands, you sinners; and purify your hearts, you double-minded." In other words, totally accept, be in complete agreement, and obey the provisions and positions of God for your life.

Second, Psalm 119:9 declares, "How can a young man cleanse his way? By taking heed according to Your word." This question is not directed only to a young man but to everyone who wants to live a pure and noble life. Rid your life, purge your life, of everything that is filthy according to the Lord, and be diligent and careful to follow the teaching and standards of God. In order for you to do this you must become a conscientious student of the Word of God.

Third, refer to Luke 11:13, "If you then, being evil, know how to give good gifts to your children, how much more will your heavenly Father give the Holy Spirit to those who ask Him!" God will give you just what you need to overcome the wiles of the devil, and that is His Holy Spirit. He will not have you floundering out there by yourself and leave you subject to Satan's schemes. As you submit to God, as you heed to His Word, His Spirit will envelope your being so that you can show the devil that you are an overcomer.

Fourth, see Mark 12:30, where Jesus declares "And you shall love the Lord your God with all your heart, with all your soul, with all your mind, and with all your strength.' This is the first commandment." This commandment summarizes all the laws of God. If you abide in His Word and allow God to work the Word in your house, in your life, it will rule your thoughts, decisions, and actions.

Our house needs to match the King's house. We need to make sure that when we rid our house, when we rid our lives, of lying, stealing, backbiting, quarreling, contrariness, idolatry, jealousy, and every evil spirit that we allow Satan and his cohorts to bring in, then we must make a full remodel and refurbish our house, our lives, to reflect the Father's house, in the name of King Jesus Christ, through the power of the Holy Spirit. We need to make sure that once our house, our lives, are completely cleansed, and even if need be, have to build from the ground up, and that our house, our lives, are full of the Spirit of God, being possessed only by Him, then we will produce the fruit of love, joy, peace, patience, kindness, goodness, faithfulness, humility, and self-control. This is all a reflection of the glory of God, which is good and right and true.

And because God loves you so much, when the renovation is complete, you won't look anything like you looked before! When the renovation is complete, you won't have the same speech you had before! When the renovation is complete, you won't walk in the same manner you did before! When the renovation is complete, you won't even have the same smile you had before! All because King Jesus changed your life! He took what was old, run down, raggedy, smelly, sin-infested, and made a complete home makeover. He saw potential in you that no one else would have ever seen. He sees you now, already, seated in the heavenly places. He sees you now as royalty. He sees you now as precious in His sight. He sees you now as lovely, beautiful, and wonderfully made. He sees you now as His masterpiece. He sees you now as His friend. He sees you now as powerful. He sees you now as mighty and strong and victorious.

The Apostle Paul teaches in Galatians 5:1 to "Stand fast therefore in the liberty wherewith Christ has made us free and be not entangled again with the yoke of bondage." Don't allow the enemy to come back in your house, to manipulate you into thinking that it is his house, after God has freed you from his bondage. Whom the Son has set free is free indeed!

CHAPTER 13

GOD IS THE DECLARATION OF TRUTH

¹⁴" But Zion said, "The Lord has forsaken me, and my Lord has forgotten me." ¹⁵ "Can a woman forget her nursing child, and not have compassion on the son of her womb? Surely, they may forget, Yet I will not forget you. ¹⁶ See, I have inscribed you on the palms of My hands; Your walls are continually before Me. ¹⁷ Your sons shall make haste; Your destroyers and those who laid you waste shall go away from you. ¹⁸ Lift up your eyes, look around and see; all these gather together and come to you. As I live," says the Lord, "You shall surely clothe yourselves with them all as an ornament and bind them on you as a bride does. ¹⁹ "For your waste and desolate places, and the land of your destruction, will even now be too small for the inhabitants; and those who swallowed you up will be far away."

Isaiah 49:14-19 (NKJV)

"We hold these truths to be self-evident, that all men are created equal. That they are endowed by their creator, with certain unalienable rights. That among these are life, liberty, and the pursuit of happiness." These are words from the preamble to the Declaration of Independence. I was in either middle school or high school when I was instructed to learn these words by heart as a part of a Social Studies class assignment. The Declaration of Independence states the principles on which our government, and our identity as Americans, are based. It is not a legally binding document. However, it is considered to be powerful and it inspires people around the world to fight for freedom and equality. President Abraham Lincoln called it "a rebuke and a stumbling-block to tyranny and oppression".

The words of this preamble were designed to convince Americans to put their lives on the line for the cause, which was to fight for security, economic stability, and identity in the separation from Britain and its king, King George III. The preamble sought to inspire and unite men through a vision of a better life.

In reality these words benefitted a certain group of people more so than others, specifically benefitting Caucasians more than enslaved Africans. We know from historical records that for over 200 years slavery was in full force, and rules and regulations that were documented did not apply to Africans. So, the truths which were to be self-evident, which were to be undisputable, which were to be undeniable for all men, were not evident for every human being.

In this chapter I'd like to review the Declaration of Independence in a different way, as I offer the declarations of Truth, from the Word of God. When I refer to the Truth, I am referring to Jesus Christ, the Anointed One in Greek, the Messiah in Hebrew, the Redeemer of all mankind, for He is the Way, the Truth, and the Life. Therefore, I'm going to provide you with declarations, statements, announcements, truths, from the Truth. John 1:1-3 tells us that "in the beginning was the Word, and the Word was with God, and the Word was God. He was in the beginning with God. All things were made through Him and without Him nothing was made that was made". In John 17:17 Jesus prayed to the Father that "He would make them (that is, His people) holy in the truth, for your word is truth". You will see in the declarations of Truth that there is independence, there is freedom, in the Truth.

Referring to our scripture text in Isaiah 49, the book is a call to the nation of Judah for them to discontinue their backsliding ways toward God, repent of their sins, return to Him for salvation, and be renewed in their spirit and in their mind. The nation of Judah had become extremely rebellious against the Lord God, for Isaiah gives them a message in chapter 1, verses 2-4, in the New Living Translation version: "Hear, O heavens! Listen, O earth! This is what the Lord says: 'the children I raised and cared for have turned against me. Even the animals, the donkey and the ox, know their owner and appreciate his care, but not my people Israel. No matter what I do for them, they still do not understand'. Oh, what a sinful nation they are! They are loaded down with a burden of guilt. They are evil and corrupt children who have turned away from the Lord. They have despised the Holy One of Israel, cutting themselves off from his help".

The people of Judah were sinning greatly against the Lord and had forsaken Him, so He brought charges against them through Isaiah. They had broken their covenant with God, laws that they promised to follow as outlined in Deuteronomy 27. They broke their promise to God and chose to carve out idols and bow to them. They broke their promise to God and chose to disregard, disrespect, and disobey their parents. They broke their promise to God and chose to steal property from their neighbors. They broke their promise to God and chose to be unjust to foreigners, orphans, and widows, and so many more commitments they chose to break in following the Lord God.

The declaration of Truth is that God despises sin and will not tolerate it. When a man or woman is deliberately practicing sin, God cannot use them. In Isaiah 65, God said that there are people who are asking about Him and looking for Him, and He is making Himself available to them. However, He has opened His arms to His own people and they constantly rebelled. They choose to follow the path of evil by worshipping and sacrificing to idols; by consulting the dead and evil spirits; by eating unclean and forbidden foods according to the law. Judah blatantly disobeyed God and still felt like they were more sacred, more holy than everyone else around them. God said that these people are "a stench in His nostrils, an acrid (or an unpleasant) smell that never goes away".

But even in His judgement, the love of God is still displayed. He said in Isaiah 48:9-10 that for His own sake, and for the honor of His name, He will hold back His anger and not wipe out Judah. God said that He has refined them but not in the way silver is refined. Rather He has refined them in the furnace of suffering, and He will rescue them for His sake. Silver is refined through an extremely heated process, much hotter than refining gold. Because of His mercy, God will not refine His people like silver, or else we most likely will not be able to sustain it.

But God will definitely refine, or purify, His people through uncomfortable processes, through afflictions brought about to remove all impurities that do not reflect the character of The Most High God. There is a Babylon that you may have to go to in order to be purified. In the King James Version of Isaiah 48:10 God said that He has "chosen you in the furnace of affliction". In other words, He is trying you, He is testing you, all while you are **in** the heat of the fire, while you are **in** your affliction, while you are **in** your hardship, while you are **in** your difficulties. The heated process is to cleanse you, to decontaminate you from sin. It is to perfect that which He has placed in you, in order for you to effectively evangelize the Gospel of Jesus Christ. Remember the three Hebrew boys who were thrown into King Nebuchadnezzar's fiery furnace, where the temperature of the heat was increased seven times greater than it was normally heated? The testing of their faith was while they were **in** the heat of the fire. God did not immediately bring them out. What God placed in them (their faith and trust in Him) was being perfected while in the midst of their affliction, to better serve Him and witness for the kingdom of God.

Refining requires fire and once the heat of the fire has been removed from the object, then all impurities will be done away with, and the object can be used properly. Accept the refining fire of God, go through the heating process, no matter how hot it gets, so that you can be used properly and effectively for the Master.

In addition to God's mercy shown in Isaiah 48, He further gives us a declaration of Truth in Isaiah 65:9, where He says that He will not destroy all of the people, for He realizes there are still some loyal servants among the defiant ones. Those He will preserve as a remnant, for them to gain His inheritance, and possess it. How merciful God is, even when we don't deserve it! How merciful God is, even in the midst of our mess! How merciful God is, even when we blatantly, deliberately walk in disobedience! What greater love is this?

Although the Lord is the God of all glory and power, the declaration of Truth is that His motivation in all He does is love. Despite the narratives that God is a narcissist, that he wants to be in control of every area of our lives, and that He is to be number one only and above all, which is true, it is the LORD's **love for us** that makes Him want us to obey and praise Him. Love's desire is that things work according to their design and purpose. We were designed and purposed to obey and praise our Creator. God calls us to submit to Him, and honor Him, for our good, not to satisfy some need in God. It is the love of God that allows His people to go through the process of the refining fires.

You who are parents understand that when you are raising your child, you have a set of do's and don'ts for them to follow. You don't hand down the rules to show who is the boss in the house, but you hand down the rules because you love them, and you want to prevent them from harm. You want your child to be steered on the right road to success. That's why you dress them in clean and proper clothes, you put them in school, you give them responsibilities around the house. It is for their future good. God is no different than our earthly parents, and even greater.

He said in Isaiah 49 that He will not forsake you nor will He forget you. Your name is inscribed on the palms of His hands. We see people today with tattoos on their bodies, as memorials for people and things that are very dear and precious to them. Well, just think about how dear and precious you are to Jesus Christ, your Savior. Your name has been imprinted, tattooed, on His nail-scarred hands. Just as He told Thomas after His resurrection to look at His hands to prove that He is the risen Messiah, so we should look to the cross, see His nail-scarred hands, and see our names tattooed on them!

What manner of love is this, that a man would lay down his life for a friend, for an infidel, for a murderer, for an adulterer, for a thief and a liar, for a sinner like you and me? With a love like this, how can He ever forget about us!

For those of you who have people speaking in your spirit that what has been lost will not be recovered, that what was ruined will not be rebuilt, that what was barren will never be fruitful, that child that left will never return, know that God is speaking a declaration of Truth to Judah in Isaiah 49:17, and He's speaking the same truth to you today: that your family, your wayward children, the backslidden spouse, everyone you've been praying for, they will make haste, in other words, they will come quickly, run swiftly, back home to the Father, referenced in the scripture as Jerusalem. God will quickly bring it to pass! And on top of that, that agent of Satan who has been trying to destroy you, trying to deconstruct what God has been constructing in your life, make you feel like you'll never get out of the desert or come up out of the valley, the declaration of Truth is that they will go away. God said it! God will cause your enemies to be humble before you and become your footstool under your feet, in the name of Jesus!

In Psalm 44:6-8 the sons of Korah sang the victorious song:

"I put no trust in my bow, my sword does not bring me victory; but you give us victory over our enemies, you put our adversaries to shame. In God we make our boast all day long, and we will praise your name forever".

Lift up your heads! Open your eyes! See the glory of the Lord all around you! Increase is on its way. Although you can't see it in the natural, see it through the eyes of the Spirit of God. They're coming! Restoration is coming! Deliverance is coming! Increase is coming! Victory is coming! Independence is coming! Freedom is coming! Liberty is coming! Healing is coming! Family is coming: Momma, Daddy, Grandma, Grandaddy, Sister, Brother, Cousins, Auntie, Uncle – they're coming! No longer have a downcast spirit! See the glory of the Lord!

The declaration of Truth is that what was once desolate and abandoned will be too small to hold the increase that's coming your way. That's what Isaiah 49:19 is telling you. Your land, your heart's desire, all your prayer requests, will soon be answered and overflowing with abundance. God's window of blessing will be opened and pour out so many blessings upon you that you will not have enough room to receive them. Notice the widow with the single jar of oil to feed her and her sons in 2 Kings 4:1-7. Ultimately, the Lord brought increase upon increase into her house as she was obedient to the word of the Lord through the prophet Elisha. But the caveat is that she acted in faith. She did not waiver. She took the word of the Lord through His prophet to be Truth.

Ruth was a non-Jewish woman, from the land of Moab, raised to worship a pagan god. She ended up marrying a man from the Israelite tribe of Judah. She became a living testimony of her faith in the God of Israel, through her relationship with her mother-in-law Naomi. And because of her faithful relationship with God, and because she abandoned the worship of her previous god, the God of Israel changed the direction of her life and brought riches to her far beyond her wildest dreams.

When Jesus was taken into custody after praying in the Garden of Gethsemane, some of His disciples thought that was the end of a wonderful relationship. When Jesus was handed over to Pilate by the chief priests and the elders to be put to death, it looked like He was certainly doomed and the Roman government would rule forever. When the decision was made for Jesus to be executed instead of Barabbas, it looked like all hope was lost. Most of the followers, the disciples of Jesus, thought that what He told them days before was just a feel-good sermon. When the execution finally took place and Jesus was crucified on Calvary's cross, people were in such despair because they thought the One they believed in, who would fulfill their dreams of freedom, was now completely annihilated.

Truth trumps everything. That is the Truth from the Word of God. The declaration of Truth is that yes, Jesus died at a site just outside Jerusalem's walls called Calvary, or Golgotha in Greek. Yes, Jesus was placed in a tomb, which was sealed, and guarded so no one would have the chance to steal his body. Yes, Jesus was mourned by so many people because they didn't understand the full viewpoint of God's plans. But the Word of God tells us that Jesus did not stay in the tomb forever, for His body to decay. The Word of God tells us that Jesus rose from the dead and was seen by many people. The declaration of Truth is that Jesus is now alive and is seated at the right-hand throne of God, making intercession for us day and night. The declaration of Truth is that "we are His people, the sheep of His pasture". We are valuable to Jesus. He takes care of us. He provides spiritual nourishment to us. He provides spiritual safety to us.

So, when you think of the preamble to the Declaration of Independence, perhaps you can think of it this way:

We (*the people of God*) hold these truths (*certainties found in the Word of God*) to be self-evident (*to be clear, definitive*) that all men are created equal (*Paul teaches us in Galatians 3:28 that "there is neither Jew nor Greek, there is neither slave nor free, there is neither male nor female; for you are all one in Christ Jesus"*), they are endowed by their Creator with certain unalienable rights (*all believers have an inheritance, an endowment, given by God, which is the right to the Tree of Life through their belief and surrender to the Lordship of Jesus Christ*), that among these (these rights) are life, liberty, and the pursuit of happiness (*once you surrender your life to the Lordship of Jesus Christ, you will have eternal life, you will experience liberty/freedom from the power of sin, and you will be happy in the Lord, as Proverbs 17:22 tells us that "A glad heart makes a healthy body, but a crushed spirit makes the bones dry"*).

CHAPTER 14
GOD REALLY LOVES YOU

"For God so loved the world that He gave His only begotten Son, that whoever believes in Him should not perish but have everlasting life."

John 3:16 (NKJV)

[22]*"Through the Lord's mercies we are not consumed, Because His compassions fail not.* [23]*They are new every morning; Great is Your faithfulness."*

Lamentations 3:22-23 (NKJV)

When a mother gives birth to her firstborn child, it's an experience she has never had before and there is nothing comparable to it. Although there was some labor throughout the pregnancy, perhaps some twists and turns emotionally as well as physically, and certainly there was much labor during the delivery of the child, the new mother realizes in the end that it was all worth it. When she holds her child in her arms for the first time, she is overwhelmed with an unexplainable amount of love she's never had for anyone in her life before.

The mother begins to make plans for this child's security throughout his childhood and perhaps even into the young adult years. She makes sure her child has a safe place to live and rest his head. She makes sure she prepares the proper food for her child to eat, to help him grow into a strong and healthy person. She makes sure her child has the proper education, teaches him right from wrong, surround him with good and positive things, and nurture the gifts she sees developing in this child. And even when this child turns into someone she didn't raise, perhaps someone who turns on her, yells at her, curses at her, disregard her feelings, in spite of all the mother has done for her child, she still forgives him. The mother doesn't disown her child. The mother doesn't throw the child away. The mother waits patiently for the child to come back to her. The mother waits patiently to hold that child in her arms again. There is nothing to be compared to the love of a mother.

But as great and precious as a mother's love, God's love is even greater and more precious than that. Just think about it. God makes daily provisions for us. God brings people into our lives that are for our good. God helps us discover the gifts he's given us and make room for them to be used among others. And in spite of all of this and more, we turn on God. We yell at Him when things don't go our way. We curse at God. We disregard His feelings, and yet, He forgives us and welcomes us back into His arms. With all of this, the message to always remember is that God really loves you.

Although you may already know that God loves you, there are times in our lives when we feel like He's forgotten all about us. When it seems like He's so far away and don't care what we're going through in our lives; when it seems like our mistakes and missteps are so tremendous that He dropped us like a bad habit, or He broke up with us like He was our boyfriend or girlfriend, and we no longer have a relationship. But God is not like man!

So, you ask yourself "how can God love me after all I've done that was so bad, so mean, so awful?" Lamentations 3:22-23 reads from the Voice Translation, "How enduring is God's loyal love, the Eternal has inexhaustible compassion. Here they are, every morning, new! Your faithfulness, God, is as broad as the day." This is called GRACE! Grace is much more than having the unmerited favor of God. For the Believer, the one who has accepted Jesus Christ as Savior, the grace of God encompasses every aspect of his life.

Now, we need to understand that everyone born under the sun have the grace of God, and that's called common grace. God's common graciousness is given to all mankind, saved and unsaved, the elect as well as the non-elect. Psalm 145:9 reads "The Lord is good to all, and His mercy is over all that He has made."

But a child of The Most High God has what is called efficacious grace and that goes well beyond what the world is privy to. Efficacious grace is God's irresistible grace, that although we were born separated from Him because of sin, He made a way to bring us back in a right relationship with Him. Although God's intention at the creation was for man to have eternal fellowship with Him, and although through Adam we rejected that offer, God's love for us was so great that He didn't reject us and throw us away. As Ephesians 2:5 reads "even when we were dead in our trespasses, He made us alive together with Christ, by grace you have been saved."

God regenerated our spirit to receive Jesus Christ as Savior and Lord.

A good illustration of this is seen in Jesus raising Lazarus from the dead. In John 11:43, it is recorded that Jesus told Lazarus to "come forth" and Lazarus came forth out of the tomb. But what had to happen before Lazarus would be able to respond to Jesus' command? Remember in this story he had been dead for several days. Lazarus had to be made alive, because a dead man cannot hear or respond! The same is true spiritually. If we are dead in our sins, as the Bible clearly teaches, then before we can respond to the gospel message and believe on the Lord Jesus Christ, we must first be made alive. Therefore, if God didn't love you, you'd still be dead in your sins and eternally lost!

Another way to know that God loves you is that He created you in His image, as He said in Genesis 1:27. This means that as a child of The Most High God you are beautiful, you are holy, you are full of goodness, you are gentle, you are loving and lovable. In spite of what negative things people say about you and no matter what negative thing you may think of yourself, you were made in God's image, which means the good work that He began in you He will perfect, He will complete, until the day of Jesus Christ. You are a work in progress, continuing to be made in His image here on Earth. He didn't say any kind of work that He began in you and then quit, but a good work He created in you that will go on and on and on until He decides the time of completion.

A third way to know that God loves you is that He is your "keeper". Psalms 121:5-7 declares "the Lord is thy keeper: the

Lord is thy shade upon thy right hand. The sun shall not smite thee by day, nor the moon by night. The Lord shall preserve thee from all evil: He shall preserve thy soul." We are also encouraged in 1 Peter 1:3-5: "Blessed be the God and Father of our Lord Jesus Christ, who according to His abundant mercy, has begotten us again to a living hope through the resurrection of Jesus Christ from the dead, to an inheritance incorruptible and undefiled and that does not fade away, reserved in heaven for you, who are kept by the power of God through faith for salvation, ready to be revealed in the last time."

In spite of all the challenges in your life God loves you so much that He is willing to keep you, to reward you with the reservation He has set aside just for you. The scripture text goes on to encourage further in verses 6 and 7 of 1 Peter 1, that in "knowing this you greatly rejoice, although you are grieved in your experiences." Tears rolling down your cheeks, popping pills to calm the anxieties, wringing your hands so hard from worrying so much – it's all to test your character in Christ, and to show who your faith and hope lies in. God takes you through these fiery difficulties to show you, you! He already knows you and already loves you, but you need to see you and understand completely what God is doing through and in you in the midst of your sufferings. He loves you so much that He knows you'll make it through all your chaos, and you will eventually meet Him in your perfect glorified body.

A fourth way to know that God loves you is just like He made a plan for Jeremiah's life while he was still in his mother's womb, God has always had a plan for your life too. Jeremiah 29:11 states "For I know the thoughts that I think toward you, thoughts of peace, and not of evil, to give you a future and a hope." There are people we tend to go to for guidance in our lives. Before I graduated I from high school I went to the school guidance counselor to get advice on career moves or suggestions. Before I graduated from college, I went the career development center to get advice on seeking jobs and organizing a good resume. Before I got married, I talked to my girlfriend and my parents about a guy I was dating who was interested in marrying me and what they thought of him. I consulted with everyone except the One I should have gone to for direction and guidance.

Just like a new mother wants her child to know her voice, God wants you to know His voice. That's why He left you His Word in order for you to know Him, to know His voice when He speaks. John 10:10 says that God wants you to have "a rich and satisfying life". It's hard to know what that looks like today with so many people talking at the same time, saying so many different things, and arguing about what is right and wrong. 2 Timothy 3 says we can know what is right and wrong, good and evil by reading God's Word. He gave you the Bible so you can know the truth, hope, and promises He offers, and He has the tools you need to live the best life possible. Jeremiah 29:13–14 states, "You will find me, if you seek me with all your heart … and I will restore your fortunes and gather you from all the nations and all the places where I have driven you." The blessing (the restoration) is directly tied to being in right relationship with God. And being in right relationship flows from seeking Him "with all your heart."

My mother used to keep a drawer full of little green booklets that were full of stamps. These books weren't anything I was allowed to play with. I couldn't use them for coloring books. I couldn't cut pages out of them to make paper dolls. They were set aside for her personal use only. At a particular time when she was ready, she would take these books to a special store where you could buy specific items. The fascinating thing about those purchases was that they weren't made with dollar bills or any coins. She would use the books with stamps in them to make the purchase. For example, if there was a set of dishes she wanted, she'd give the store clerk maybe 10 of the stamped-filled books. If she wanted a cup and saucer set she might give the clerk 5 books. Whatever she wanted she had to have the stamp-filled books that equaled the amount charged for the item. The little booklets were called Greenbax stamped books. A specific amount of stamped-filled books were exchanged for a desired item.

While keeping this illustration in mind, I want you to know that the love of God is so great towards you that He doesn't accept just any exchange for our lives. Money won't do it. We see that in the confrontation between Peter and the sorcerer Simon, who wanted to buy the free gift of salvation and the indwelling of the Holy Spirit for his personal gain. We know that God will not accept the blood of animals. Old Testament law was specific of the type of animal to be sacrificed and what was accepted by God for the people's atonement. But thanks be unto God, we are no longer subject to the Old Testament law of animal sacrifices. There was only one means of payment and that was by the sacrificial blood of Jesus Christ! He showed you how much He loves you by what He endured in the Garden of Gethsemane, the agony of the presence of hell on your behalf, what He had to experience for you, for me, for all of us, so we wouldn't have to. He showed you how much He loves you by what He endured on Calvary's cross. He separated Himself from The Father, from God, on your behalf. He took the penalty of sin and hell on your behalf! Hebrews 9:26b tells us clearly that "Jesus appeared once at the end of the ages to get rid of sin by sacrificing Himself."

There are so many more, countless ways to know that God loves us. But as mentioned earlier, there are times when we don't feel close to Him, when we feel all alone, when life really hits us in the face. So, what do we do when we get that feeling?

#1 – Get some rest.

The world looks darkest when we're exhausted. Certainly, Elijah was extremely tired and felt so alone from running away from Jezebel in 1 Kings 19, so tired that he wanted the Lord to take his life. You will more likely see things a little differently after some rest.

#2 – Remember what God has already done in your life.

Psalm 77:10-12 states "I will appeal to this, to the years of the right hand of The Most High. I will remember the deeds of the Lord, yes, I will remember your wonders of old. I will ponder all your work and meditate on your mighty deeds." We tend to focus on what's right in front of us but take the time to remember what is behind you as well.

#3 – You can make a conscious choice to leave your case in God's hands.

God knows that we are only human, as Psalm 103:14 so compassionately points out, that "He knows our frame, He remembers that we are dust." Know that He will not let you fall, no matter what your feelings may say. Only in Christ are His promises "yes and amen", as taught in 2 Corinthians 1:20.

So, now that you know God really loves you, why not follow 2 Corinthians 7:1, and that is to "cleanse yourself from anything that contaminates your body or spirit so that you make your holiness complete in the fear of God." Now that you know that God really loves you, why not remember Romans 8:35, which asks the question "who will separate you from Christ's love? Will you be separated by trouble, or distress, or harassment, or famine, or nakedness, or danger, or sword? As it is written, 'we are being put to death all day long for your sake. We are treated like sheep for slaughter.' But in all these things we win a sweeping victory through the One who loved us." Now that you know God really loves you, why not remember His promise in 2 Corinthians 2:14, that "He always causes you to triumph in Christ."

We all have longed for that someone, that relationship, that would provide us with security and safety, someone who would protect us from harm and danger, to defend and care for us on a continual basis. Jesus is the only one who can provide all these qualities and much more. It's absolutely wonderful to know there is comfort in the Word of God, as it tells us the Lord provides the security, the safety, the protection, and the covering we desire. He keeps us from hurt, harm and danger, and He is our defense in every situation because He loves and cares for us. He is our keeper and only He can keep us in the way that we need to be kept. David said in Psalm 3:3 that the Lord is "a shield for me, my Glory and the lifter-up of my head."

Know that the Lord is always with us without ceasing, consistently and constantly there. This means that He remains the same, He never changes, always faithful and ever present. He said He would never leave us nor forsake us. He's concerned about our well-being. He knows all about us, our concerns, our anxieties, our worries, our ups, our downs, our triumphs, our joys, our coming in and our going out and yet, He sustains and preserves us through them all. No earthly person can keep your soul or care for you in the manner in which the Lord does, and not just in the right now, but at all times and forevermore! He is in the business of keeping folk, just look at the Israelites. They know about being kept by God and God has made these same promises to us as well today.

CHAPTER 15
WHO IS GOD TO YOU?

¹²"So He (God speaking to Moses) said, "I will certainly be with you. And this shall be a sign to you that I have sent you: When you have brought the people out of Egypt, you shall serve God on this mountain. ¹³Then Moses said to God, "Indeed, when I come to the children of Israel and say to them, 'The God of your fathers has sent me to you,' and they say to me, 'What is His name?' what shall I say to them? ¹⁴And God said to Moses, "I AM WHO I AM." And He said, "Thus you shall say to the children of Israel, 'I AM has sent me to you.'

Exodus 3:12-14 (NKJV)

We have so many things pulling at us every day of our lives: our children need our attention; husbands or wives need a loving stroke; the boss has a deadline you must meet; your friend needs a shoulder to cry on. But what about you? What do you need? During your personal times of difficulty, times when you need a loving stroke, a shoulder to cry on, just a friend who will be your confidant, who is God is to you? Even during the holiday seasons when families come together, laugh, play, enjoy each other's company. But there are so many who don't have these joyful experiences. So, the question becomes, "what and who do you need God to be in your life?"

The scripture reference in Exodus lets us know that God is self-existent, meaning He has His being of Himself, and He has no dependence on any other. He is all-sufficient, meaning He is the inexhaustible fountain of being and blessedness. He is eternal, absolute, and unchangeable, the same yesterday, today, and forever, as Hebrew 13:8 declares.

When we hear God describe himself as "I AM THAT I AM", what He is saying more deeper is that "I will be what I am", as well as "I am what I will be", and that He is even "I will be what I will be". This is in contrast to others which declare that they are, and have been, and shall be, because what they have been might have been otherwise, and what they are might possibly not have been at all, and what they shall be may be very different from what now is. Therefore, they are changeable, dependent, and in essence, are insecure and ineffective, which means today they may be one thing, tomorrow another thing, and the next day possibly nothing at all.

We need to understand that God doesn't have an identity problem. He knows who He is. But the question is, do you know who He is? Because what He represents to you in your life is how you will define Him to your friends, families, business associates, etc. Do you respect Him? Are you in awe of Him? Do you truly fear Him? When God tells Moses about Himself in Exodus 3:6 "I am the God of your fathers, the God of Abraham, Isaac and Jacob", He just may be reminding Moses, "I have written an autobiography about myself. Remember what I've said and what I've done throughout history. Then you know something about Me and will be ready to understand the meaning and intent of this personal experience."

Who is God to you? What personal experience have you had with him to declare who He absolutely is in your life? How can you recognize or understand God's meaning in an experience if you are unfamiliar with who He says He is? Here are a few suggestions to offer as you evaluate your experiences with God.

First and foremost, He is Elohim, the Supreme God. The one and only true and living God. He is Elohim who created the heavens and the earth. He is the one of strength, all-powerful, infinite, and who shows that He is the sustainer, creator, and supreme judge of the whole world. In Him we live, we move, and have our being. All of our strength and mobility come from Elohim. The very breath in our bodies come from Elohim. We are absolutely dependent on Him for every aspect of our lives.

Secondly, you can know God as Jehovah Nissi, your Banner, the one who will fight your battle for you. The evidence is found in Exodus 17:8-16, where the men of Amalek came to war against the Israelites. Moses told Joshua to get the best men from the Israelites to sign up for war, and Joshua did. Moses went on top of a nearby hill with Aaron and Hur to watch the battle. As long as Moses held his hands up with the same staff he used from God to guide the Israelites across the Red Sea, the men of Israel were winning the war against the Amalekites. But whenever Moses lowered his hands, the Amalekites took advantage. After some time, Moses' grew weary and tired. So Aaron and Hur took a stone and put it under Moses, and he sat on it. Then Aaron and Hur held up Moses' hands, one on one side, and the other on the other side. Therefore, his hands were steady until sunset. Eventually Joshua and the men of Israel defeated the Amalekites with the sword. And verses 14-16 reads: "Then the Lord said to Moses, "Write this as a memorial in a book and recite it in the ears of Joshua, that I will utterly blot out the memory of Amalek from under heaven." And Moses built an altar, a memorial of thanksgiving to God, and called the name of it, JEHOVAH-NISSI, The Lord Is My Banner, saying, "A hand upon the throne of the Lord! The Lord will have war with Amalek from generation to generation." This is a testament that when we go through a struggle in our lives, Jehovah Himself is our protection, our banner, and in Him we are conquerors! Therefore, we declare 2 Timothy 1:7 which states "for God has not given us the spirit of fear but of power, and of love, and a sound mind, or self-control. Because the Lord is your Banner, "you can do all things through Christ who strengthens you", as Philippians 4:13 teaches us.

Then you can also know God as Jehovah Raah, the Lord my Shepherd. The first verse of the 23rd Psalm declares, "The Lord is my Shepherd, I shall not want", or as written in the Septuagint, the Greek Old Testament, "The Lord shepherds me". The chief meaning of Jehovah is derived from the Hebrew word "Havah", which means "to be", or "to exist". It also suggests that He is "to become known", indicating Jehovah as the God who reveals Himself unceasingly, intimately as a friend. Therefore, Raah can be translated as the "Lord my Friend". Just as a good shepherd lays down his life to defend the sheep that are entrusted to him, so Jesus is our Good Shepherd, our True Friend, who laid down His life for those whom God entrusted to Him, which is the whole world, to remove the penalty of sin from our soul. Jesus stated in John 15:13-16, "Greater love has no man than this, that one should lay down his life for his friends. You are my friends if you do what I command you. No longer do I call you servants, for the servant does not know what his master is doing; but I have called you friends, for all that I have heard from my Father I have made known to you."

As best of friends we could have in this life, it is extremely rare to have a friend who would sacrifice his or her life for someone else's to the degree which Jesus gave His. We're not talking about what someone would do in some extraordinary or unexpected danger, or on a sudden alarm, but someone who would voluntarily and deliberately do so, in the coolest moment, submit to laying down his or her life for the preservation and happiness of another. And because He did this, we can call Him Jehovah Raah, our Good Shepherd, because there is nothing in this world that we have need of that He will not provide. And if we don't have everything we desire, we can conclude that it's either not fit for us or good for us to have, or we shall have it in due time. He is Jehovah Raah.

God can also be known as Jehovah Shammah, the Lord is present, or the Lord my companion. Zechariah was a prophet and priest of God who was born in Babylon during the Israelites' captivity there. The new king of Babylon, King Cyrus of Persia, made a decree that all enslaved Israelites were allowed to return home to Jerusalem. Although freedom had finally come, not everyone was willing to leave Babylon.

Some of the Israelites had become comfortable in the security and wealth they've come to know. Zechariah, as well as his partner Haggai during this time, tried to compel the Israelites to leave Babylon because they would ultimately be destroyed with the city. Although God banished the Israelites to Babylon because of their disobedience towards Him, He declared their time of punishment was over, and He wanted to renew their relationship with them. He wanted them to know that He saw their pain and anguish, and believed they learned their lesson and was ready for reconciliation.

In Zechariah 2:7-11, we read the words of the Lord through his prophet Zechariah, instructing the people of Israel to leave Babylon: "Up, up! Flee from the land of the north," says the Lord; "for I have spread you abroad like the four winds of heaven," says the Lord. Up, Zion! Escape, you who dwell with the daughter of Babylon. For thus says the Lord of hosts: "He sent Me after glory, to the nations which plunder you; for he who touches you touches the apple of His eye. For surely, I will shake My hand against them, and they shall become spoil for their servants. Then you will know that the Lord of hosts has sent Me. Sing and rejoice, O daughter of Zion! For behold, I am coming, and I will dwell in your midst," says the Lord. Many nations shall be joined to the Lord in that day, and they shall become My people. And I will dwell in your midst. Then you will know that the Lord of hosts has sent Me to you."

God is faithful towards His children, and no matter where we are, God is ever-present. Even when we're in the gutter most part of life, God is Jehovah-Shammah, our Companion. And even today, He is calling some of you back to Him. He knows where you've been, He knows the pain of it all, and He's been there with you the whole time - ever-present.

Lastly you can know God as Abba Father. Abba is how Jesus addressed His Father in the Aramaic language, and it was a common term in those days, used to express affection, confidence, and trust. Abba signifies the close, intimate relationship of a father and his child, just as a young child would put his complete trust in his "daddy". The only persons we see in scripture having called God Abba Father were Jesus Christ and the Apostle Paul. Both had very significant yet different experiences in their personal relationships with God. On one hand we have the Savior of the world, having come to draw all men to God. On the other hand, we have a man who was determined to destroy the belief in Jesus and all He stood for. Two entirely different men, but yet God brought them together in such a miraculous way, and they both changed the course of the world in the knowledge of God. Through seen and unseen danger, through difficulties and hardships, these men drew closer to God and developed such an intimate relationship with Him that they were able to call him Abba Father without hesitation.

So, when we call God Abba Father, we are putting more emphasis on the fatherhood of God. Yes, He's your Father, but He can also be your Daddy, your Papa, your Leader, your Protector, your Rescuer. Yes, He can even be your Craftsman because He knows you more than you know yourself and handcrafted your personality before you were a twinkle in your parents' eyes.

These names of God are just a sample of a long list of other identifications for Him. We can pick from any one on that list and still come out with the perfect essence of His character. From the list you could choose Him as your Jehovah Rapha, the God who heals, having healed you from a disease that caused doctors to be dumbfounded and didn't know what course of action to take that would bring deliverance.

From that list, He could be chosen as Jehovah Shalom, the God of Peace. When your world has turned upside down and you've gotten to the point where you don't know which way is up, you clearly heard him speak to your spirit and said "peace, be still, know that I am God". That's the God of Peace.

From that list He could be Jehovah Jireh, the Lord who provides. When you get between a rock and a hard place like Brother Abraham, ready to be obedient to God and sacrifice his one and only son, trusting that God will step in right on time, you will learn like he did, that God is the ultimate provider, and will do the same for you. You may have lost your job and you're the only source of income for your family but know that God is able to do exceedingly abundantly above all you can ask or think according to the power that works in you.

If nothing else, go back to the beginning and say that He is to you I AM THAT I AM. God is everything. He is the air that you breathe. He is the song that you sing. He is your best friend, your confidant. He is your joy even in the midst of sorrow. He is your hope for a better day tomorrow. You can rest assured that He loves you unconditionally. You can look to Him as being your Redeemer, the One who gave His life for you. The One who sacrificed His all, on Calvary's tree, on a hill called Golgotha, just to save you. You can look to Him as being the One who makes you whole, and to Him you are not only good, but very good, as the scripture says that everything He made was very good. There are really no words that can truly articulate His nature, His awesomeness, how great He is. It's just enough to say that He is God and there is no other God besides Him!

Just think about it once again as you ask yourself the question, who is God to you? How well do you know God? When you feel the cool breeze from a soft wind, who is God to you? When you see the lightning flash in the sky and hear the thunder roar, who is God to you? When you see senseless killing on the news programs, still who is God to you? When special relationships have come to an end, still who is God to you? Just look at your personal history with God and remember what He told Moses in Exodus 3:6, "I am the God of your father, the God of Abraham, Isaac and Jacob", then you should be able to answer the question of who God is to you.

CONCLUSION

23"Thus says the L<small>ORD</small>: "Let not the wise man glory in his wisdom, let not the mighty man glory in his might, nor let the rich man glory in his riches; 24 But let him who glories glory in this, that he understands and knows Me, that I am the L<small>ORD</small>, exercising lovingkindness, judgment, and righteousness in the earth. For in these I delight," says the L<small>ORD</small>."

Jeremiah 9:23–24 (NKJV)

The Apostle Paul subordinated everything in his life to one goal: "that I may know Him" (Philippians 3:10). This greatest of all the apostles counted everything else in life as *skor*, "dung," compared to "the surpassing value of knowing Christ Jesus my Lord" (Philippians 3:8). There is no higher knowledge in life than the knowledge of God. It is God's desire that we understand Him and that this understanding give us the courage to conquer, as the heroes of Hebrews 11 conquered, by seeing Him who is unseen (Hebrews 11:27). As we learn to concentrate our thoughts on the essence and the attributes of God rather than on ourselves and our circumstances, we gradually come to realize that we could not possibly ever have a problem that He cannot solve. We begin to understand that we do not always have to know what God is doing. We only have to know that He knows what He is doing.

As mentioned in chapter one, the essence of God is the fundamental nature of who He is and His essence, His attributes, and His character, which are ever present in the Christian's life. In conclusion, here are a few powerful features of who we can depend on Him to be:

1. Sovereign

³⁴"And at the end of the time I, Nebuchadnezzar, lifted my eyes to heaven, and my understanding returned to me; and I blessed The Most High and praised and honored Him who lives forever: For His dominion is an everlasting dominion, and His kingdom is from generation to generation. ³⁵ All the inhabitants of the earth are reputed as nothing; He does according to His will in the army of heaven and among the inhabitants of the earth. No one can restrain His hand or say to Him, "What have You done?"

Daniel 4:34–35 (NKJV)

God's divine will is above every will. He always has everything under control. He, as Creator, is King, Ruler over all His creation. He has assigned to every living thing its place in the universe and the scope of its freedom and authority. If we know this to be true, then we should be able, in the midst of the most difficult circumstances, in the darkest times of our lives, to give thanks to Him. Only when we acknowledge His sovereignty and yield ourselves to it can we rest, knowing that we occupy the only safe place in the universe, the center of His will.

2. Righteous

"The Lord is righteous in all His ways, gracious in all His works."

Psalm 145:17 (NKJV)

God is absolute righteousness, perfect goodness. It is impossible for Him to do anything wrong. He is holy and free from sin or wrong. He is guiltless. He is absolutely righteous both in His person and in His ways. He cannot look upon or have fellowship with that which is anything less than absolute righteousness. Because He is perfect and right, His plan is perfect and right. If we understand this, then we should realize that whatever He does or allows in our lives is perfect because it is part of His perfect plan and His perfect person. If we know that He can never make a mistake with us, we can be thankful in all things.

3. Just

"He is the Rock, His work is perfect; for all His ways are justice, a God of truth and without injustice; righteous and upright is He."

Deuteronomy 32:4 (NKJV)

God is absolutely just. It is impossible for Him to do anything unfair. By virtue of His being the Creator, God has the absolute right of authority over His creatures. He has given to man fair and righteous laws which every one of us has broken. God's righteousness demands that disobedience against His laws be punished. God's justice fulfilled that demand when God the Son on the cross took the punishment for all men's sin and disobedience. Because of this, God is just (fair and right) to forgive anyone who accepts Christ's provision. He is also just to condemn anyone who rejects His provision. God's justice will see to it that everything that falls in line with His righteousness will be blessed and everything that does not will be cursed. Understanding God's justice should not only give us the constant assurance that even if the world treats us unfairly, God never will. But it should also remind us that He, who is the only one who knows all the facts, will always discipline the unbelief and reward the faith of His children in His perfect time.

4. Love

"He who does not love does not know God, for God is love.";

1 John 4:8 (NKJV)

"He who does not love does not know God, for God is love."

1 John 4:16 (NKJV)

Agape, the love that is part of the essence of God, is nothing like the love that man produces. God's love is part of His eternal Being and thus can never be increased, diminished, or changed. Long before God created anything, love existed among the three Persons of the Trinity. The love that God extends to man is an impersonal love in the sense that it is not based on the goodness or integrity of the person who is the object of love, but on the goodness and integrity of God. God does not love us because of who we are, but because of who He is. The love of God extended to man is not an emotion or a feeling. It is a divine passion for the ultimate good of men. It is not passive; it is active. It is not casual; it is sacrificial. God's love is exemplified in John 3:16 ("For God so loved the world that He gave His only begotten Son, that whoever believes in Him should not perish but have everlasting life.") and Romans 5:8 ("But God demonstrates His own love toward us, in that while we were still sinners, Christ died for us."). God Himself was the initiator. He made the ultimate sacrifice not for those who were eager and ready to know and serve Him, but for those in rebellion, for enemies. If we understand this love of God, we know that no matter how lonely or isolated or forsaken we may feel, God loves us. If God is love, then whatever happens to us is an expression of His love.

5. Eternal Life

"Now to the King eternal, immortal, invisible, to God who alone is wise, be honor and glory forever and ever. Amen."

1 Timothy 1:17 (NKJV)

God always has existed and always will exist. He is the source of all life. He is not subject to time, because He existed before time was and is, in fact, the inventor of time. Therefore, God always sees everything from the eternal perspective. He always has our welfare in view, not only for time but also for eternity. If we understand this, we can be thankful under any circumstances because we know absolutely that God is working for our eternal good.

6. Omniscient

"For if our heart condemns us, God is greater than our heart, and knows all things."

1 John 3:20 NKJV

All knowledge belongs to God. He knows everything past, present, and future, everything actual and everything possible. He also understands all things. He has known and understood everything forever. He cannot be confused or surprised. Nothing is news to God. If we understand that God is omniscient, then we will always know that a wisdom greater than our own is in control of circumstances and situations. We will always know where to go with our questions and problems.

7. Omnipotent

"And I heard, as it were, the voice of a great multitude, as the sound of many waters and as the sound of mighty thunderings, saying, "Alleluia! For the Lord God Omnipotent reigns!"

Revelations 19:6 NKJV

God is infinitely, awesomely powerful. He is able to accomplish anything that He wills, but He never abuses His power, and He never wills to accomplish anything contrary to His holy nature. If we understand this, then we need never doubt His ability to keep His promises, to answer our prayers, or to carry out His plan. We can be thankful in the face of our own weakness, because we know His strength.

8. Omnipresent

"Can anyone hide himself in secret places, so I shall not see him?" says the Lord; "Do I not fill heaven and earth?" says the Lord."

Jeremiah 23:24 NKJV

God is always in all places. He fills the entire universe. This means He can see and hear everything all the time and is always present in every circumstance of our lives. Because God is omnipotent and omnipresent and independent of time, He always has time for everyone. He can give full attention to each of us as if we were the only person on earth. If we understand this, then we know with absolute certainty that we are never alone, never outside the sphere of His care.

9. Immutable

"Jesus Christ is the same yesterday, today, and forever."

Hebrews 13:8 NKJV

God has never changed and will never change. He can neither increase nor decrease. His essence and attributes will always remain the same, no matter what. If we understand this, then we can rest in the fact that no matter how inconsistent or unstable or undependable we are, God will always be consistent, stable, and dependable. When we feel like He no longer loves us or does not understand us or cannot help us, we can ignore our feelings because we know the fact of His immutability.

10. Veracity

"For the word of the Lord is right, and all His work is done in truth."

Psalm 33:4 NKJV

Because God is truth itself, He always acts in veracity ("devotion to the truth or truthfulness") and in faithfulness toward man. Because it is impossible for God to lie, we know that His every word to us is true. The Bible is God's revelation of truth to man. We can always depend on His Word. If we know that God is true and that His Word is true, and if we claim His promises, then the essence of God will become a source of encouragement to us. We will be able to pray in faith, to pray without ceasing, and to pray with thanksgiving.

Although no creature can define what God is, because He is incomprehensible and dwelling in inaccessible light, yet it has pleased His Majesty to reveal Himself to us in his Word, so far as our weak capacity can best conceive Him. Thus, God is that one spiritual and infinitely perfect essence, whose being is of Himself eternal.

Ephesians 4:4 states that "you were called to one hope when you were called", and that one hope is in one Spirit, the Spirit of God the Father, The Godhead of the Trinity, the Spirit of His Son Jesus Christ, and His Holy Spirit, which His presence is abiding in every believer today. This is in contrast to what the world is relaying to everyone, that there are various ways to know God. Christians were called to be apologists for the Gospel of Jesus Christ, one who defends the one and only true, infallible, living Word of God in all manners of life.

Christians were not called to be a part of the popular, acceptable beliefs of today. They were not called to be a polytheist, one who believes in multiple gods. I remember when I was in high school we had to study mythology, studying various Greek gods: Zeus-the god of the sky; Apollo-the god of music, poetry, art, prophecy, truth, archery, plague, healing, sun and light; Aphrodite- the goddess of beauty and love;

and <u>Poseidon</u>-the god of the sea, earthquakes, and horses. The believer was called into one hope in God. How can you have hope in mythical, fairy-tale gods?

Christians were not called to be a pantheist, one whose view is that God is everything and everyone, and that everyone and everything is God. To be a pantheist is similar to being a polytheist but goes further in that pantheism teaches that everything is God. For example, a tree is God, a rock is God, an animal is God, the sky is God, the sun is God, even you are God! Why would I have hope in an inanimate object like a tree or a rock? Why should I put my hope in another man as my god when he is just as imperfect as I am?!

Christians were called to be a monotheist, a person who worships only one God while denying the existence of other gods. They have been called into a divine relationship with one God. He's called Jehovah, Adonai, Lord, Master. He's called El Shaddai, God Almighty; El Elyon, God Most High; El Olam, The Everlasting God.

Yes, He has many names, but He is still one God whose many names describe His nature, His character, His essence. His names reveal who He is and who He can be to us in so many ways throughout our relationship. He is still the one God, the one Savior, the one Spirit, who is the only one who can take away the sins of the world and throw them into the sea of forgetfulness. He is the only one who has called every man out of the darkness and deceptions of this world, so that he can walk in the marvelous light of salvation, relinquishing sin and follow after Jesus Christ.

There will always be people who will doubt the existence of God and all that He was in the past, is in the present, and will be in the future. However, that doesn't negate the fact that He is God and that He is absolute. The skeptics cannot disprove the fact that God is in all and over all things that exist. Through Him all things were made and without Him nothing was made that has been made.

The Word of God teaches in Ephesians 4:13 that the will of the Father for the body of Christ is that we all reach unity in the faith and in the knowledge of His Son Jesus Christ, and that we all would become mature, reaching the whole measure of the fullness of Christ, to truly and fully walk in the characteristic of the image of God. This the responsibility of the Church before the skeptics of the world, to show them the image and essence of God as we walk after His likeness, to shine the light of Christ before all men, and Jesus said, "then, will I draw all men unto me" (John 12:32).

RESOURCES

Holy Bible, New King James Version (NKJV)

Holy Bible, New Living Translation (NLT)

Holy Bible, Amplified Version (AMP)

Holy Bible, The Voice Translation (VOICE)

Holy Bible, The Good News Translation (GNT)

Holy Bible, God's Word Translation (GW)

https://www.christianitytoday.com/biblestudies/articles/evangelism/seven-questions-skeptics-ask.html

https://www2.gracenotes.info/topics/essence-single-column.html

The Essence of God – Basic Training Bible Ministries - https://basictraining.org/the-essence-of-god/

https://www.goodreads.com/quotes/452317-keep-your-face-to-the-sunshine-and-you-cannot-see

https://www.preceptaustin.org/gospel_of_john-f_b_meyer-3

What is pantheism? | GotQuestions.org - https://www.gotquestions.org/pantheism.html

Christian Hymn: "My Hope Is Built on Nothing Less" by Edward Mote, a pastor at Rehoboth Baptist Church in Horsham, West Sussex.

https://efhutton.com

Enduring Word Bible Commentary Mark Chapter 1 - https://enduringword.com/bible-commentary/mark-1/

Donald Whitney, Author and Professor

Southern Baptist Theological Seminary in Louisville, Kentucky

God's Essence (embracedbytruth.com) -

http://embracedbytruth.com/God/God's Essence/God's Essence.html

About The Author
Dr. Marie Burkins

Reverend Doctor Marie Burkins is a native of Meridian, MS and raised in Charleston, SC. She was educated in the school systems of Kittery, Maine; Charleston, SC; and Goose Creek, SC. Dr. Burkins has been married for 39 years to Mr. Ronald Burkins and they are the proud parents of two children: Victoria Marie and William Edward Jeroy.

Dr. Burkins earned an Associate Degree in Business Administration from Trident Technical College in N. Charleston, SC. She has also earned degrees in Associate of Arts in Ministry, Bachelor of Arts in Ministry, and Master of Arts in Theology, all from The Word of God Bible Institute in Columbia, SC, under the auspices of The International College of Ministry in Orlando, FL. Dr. Burkins has also earned a Doctor of Theology Degree from The Bethesda Theological Seminary in Columbia, SC, where she is an Adjunct Professor and a member of their Advisory Board. Dr. Burkins is a certified teacher with the Accrediting Commission International, Inc.

Dr. Burkins is a member of Zion Canaan Baptist Church in Columbia, SC and among the many positions she's held, she is currently serving as the Church Administrator, the Director of the Maturity Team/Christian Education Department, Sunday School and Bible Study Teacher, and Chaplain of the

Women's Auxiliary of the Gethsemane Missionary Baptist Association.

Dr. Burkins' favorite scripture is 2 Corinthians 5:7 – "For we walk by faith, not by sight", because her trust, her confidence, her dependence, and her reliance is completely in God, and God alone.

www.ingramcontent.com/pod-product-compliance
Lightning Source LLC
LaVergne TN
LVHW072050060526
838201LV00029B/325/J